MIMESIS
INTERNATIONAL

AESTHETICS
n. 9

GIOIA LAURA IANNILLI

THE AESTHETICS OF EXPERIENCE DESIGN

A Philosophical Essay

MIMESIS
INTERNATIONAL

© 2020 – MIMESIS INTERNATIONAL (Milano – Udine)
www.mimesisinternational.com
e-mail: info@mimesisinternational.com

Book series: *Aesthetics*, n. 9

Isbn: 9788869772986

© MIM Edizioni Srl
P.I. C.F. 02419370305

TABLE OF CONTENTS

For M.

ACKNOWLEDGMENTS

This project would never have been possible without the contribution of many people. In particular, I would like to thank Gustavo Marfia (University of Bologna), both for providing useful suggestions and comments on an early draft of the essay, when it was an entry for the *International Lexicon of Aesthetics*, and for concretely introducing me to VARLAB (Virtual and Augmented Reality Lab at the Department for Life Quality Studies, University of Bologna), where I had the opportunity to immersively experience the potential of digital technologies. I am equally indebted to Markus Ahola (Experience Platform at Aalto University, Espoo), who has been an important interlocutor during the past months starting from the same text. As a professional experience designer, he has been able to explain some technical aspects of the discipline that otherwise would still be unclear to me. It goes without saying that I am grateful to Simona Chiodo (Polytechnic University of Milan) and Tonino Griffero (University of Rome "Tor Vergata") for providing useful advice, and to Stefano Marino (University of Bologna) for his always friendly and fundamental help in particular with this manuscript. I am thankful for the Summer conversations at the American Institute of Philosophical and Cultural Thought in Murphysboro, Illinois, with Randy Auxier (Southern Illinois University Carbondale) and John R. Shook (Bowie State University, Maryland). This latter kindly contributed to the proofreading process. My gratitude goes also to Nicholas Guardiano, whose assistance and friendship at the Special Collections Research Center of the Morris Library (Southern Illinois University Carbondale), and honest criticism on some parts of the essay have been more than useful. I cannot thank enough Larry Hickman (Southern Illinois University Carbondale) who, since last Summer, when I had the honor to meet him, has been kindly reading and providing precious comments on my research on John Dewey. Over the last four years I have benefited greatly from discussions with Ossi Naukkarinen (Aalto University, Espoo) who, also by raising insightful questions and providing insightful remarks after reading this essay, has once again showed me that things can and should be kept together nicely. My deepest gratitude goes to Giovanni Matteucci (University of Bologna) who, since the beginning, has been more than a "gentle nudge", patiently and generously orienting my research and introducing me to the philosophy of John Dewey and Theodor W. Adorno. I thank him for sharing with me aspects that otherwise would have remained unnoticed. Last but not least I would like to thank all those "operators of the implicit" who are with me everyday, and my very own experience designer, Linda Gioia Penna.

INTRODUCTION

The first few months of 2020 have had perhaps an unprecedented impact on the whole world. They called for the need to re-understand the limits and possibilities offered by our present and particular life context. A time when many of the cornerstones of the globalized experience, at least as they have been effortlessly experienced in recent decades, have been dismantled. Our sense of identity, belonging, security, normality and planning has been tested greatly.

In these same months and independent of the global emergency just mentioned, this same set of themes has been addressed along different lines in two fields of the creative and cultural industry such as fashion and advertising linked in particular to mobility. These are fields which, today more than ever before, must find new ways of managing, producing and distributing their products and offers suitable for the new context that we are facing.

In the first case I am referring to Balenciaga's show during Paris Fashion Week. The theme addressed for the Winter collection by the creative director of the Spanish fashion house, Demna Gvasalia, is in fact climate change. The show's venue is a multi-sensory and immersive scenario, featuring music that alternates between dark, pressing, quiet and in some ways motivational tones; images of natural and anthropic phenomena fleeting on the ceiling of the venue and reflected on the water levels that flood both the catwalk — through which the models walk undaunted — and the first rows of seats in the audience thus rendered unusable. The collection includes garments ranging from football and clerical uniforms, which seem to evoke a sense of belonging and identity, to biker gear and other garments made from waterproof and protective materials that seem to evoke a sense of security. Many of the models in the show wear earpods or carry smartphones so they seem connected, and in the course of the show the number of those who carry a bag or duffel bag among them increases, as if preparing for an escape elsewhere. An elsewhere that at the end of the show can be glimpsed in a new line of the horizon. A new planet, perhaps, or our old world seen with renewed eyes, or better perceived with renewed senses.

In a second case I refer to an advertisement created for the Scandinavian airline *SAS*. This commercial approaches the theme of national identity in a decidedly anti-essentialist way, as "nothing original" and immutable, but as something procedural and forged intersubjectively, and going also beyond its own borders. This commercial, not by chance, has caused the airline to receive strong criticism from anti-immigration and far-right parties. The following excerpt provides a clear summary of the company's corporate policy:

> We take everything we like on our trips abroad, adjust it a little bit and it's a unique Scandinavian thing. Going out into the world inspires us to think big, even though we are quite small, because every time we go beyond our borders we add colors, innovation, progress, adding the best of anywhere to here.

This *SAS* narrative is a subtle play of balances between different instances that with the proper contribution of "color", innovation and progress get the best out of situations and create a personal but shared "here": that is, of identity, belonging, stability.

In both cases we are dealing with the ability of creative teams to use their imaginative sensibilities, but also their planning and organizational skills, making concrete or even only evoking possible, tendential and potential scenarios; their perceptual sensibilities, grasping processes that are already in place in our reality materially, and therefore historically; their expressive sensibilities, appealing to the sensibilities of others.

In both cases we are dealing with the evident overcoming of the dichotomy between a so-called usefulness (i.e. market, efficiency of the fashion and global tourism system, clothing, transportation systems), and a so-called uselessness (i.e. imaginative construction, narration, status-symbol, lifestyle), elements that, instead, in the current experience, are finely intertwined.

In both cases we are dealing with experiences of a common world carried out by common individuals that have been processed and rendered in more perspicuous and conspicuous ways, re-issued in that same world and re-experienced in the first person.

In both cases we have to do with ways of making something experienceable, of designing something not yet thematized, or rather, something not yet thematized in a certain way, by intensifying aspects that make it something present, something personal.

Beyond any easy and perhaps inappropriate rhetoric, this is what the phenomenon at the center of the present analysis, Experience Design, tends to do.

Experience Design is going to be discussed from the point of view of the competences involved to ensure its success, whether we are talking about producers' or users'; from the point of view of a reconsideration of the relationship between function and form in a processual and relational sense; from the point of view of the analysis of the configuration modalities of cohesive nuclei, or kernels of meaningfulness and gratification in which things are kept together and work.

This essay is divided into three chapters. The first one is devoted to the historical-conceptual reconstruction of the Experience Design phenomenon and to an initial theoretical proposal fostering a specifically aesthetic conception of it. This chapter may sometimes sound like a manifesto. The hope, however, is that this will not be perceived as a prescriptive and essentialist attitude in the treatment of the phenomenon under analysis, but as the necessarily positive tone of a first exploration which, as such, sometimes has the character of heuristicity and of tentativeness. However, this tone will be balanced, near the end of the chapter, by a series of critical questions to which we will try to answer in the two following chapters. The latter are more explicitly theoretical and philosophical, and address the perspectives of two classics of contemporary philosophy such as John Dewey and Theodor W. Adorno with respect to themes that are tangent or at least resonant with those at the center of this philosophical essay.

This essay evidently does not deal with what has now become our problematic life context, not least because it was conceived before such a phase. However, the aim of this essay, from the beginning, is to provide a questioning reading, from a specifically aesthetic point of view, of the relationship between individuals and the strongly structured, designed experiential contexts in which the former move about every day. Its intent is to show how, thanks also to the contribution of an aesthetic point of view, it is possible to bring forth the irreducibility of that sense of humanity that is sometimes believed to be lost in these contexts.

At the heart of this will be a basic question: to what extent and under what conditions is it possible to consider Experience Design a truly aesthetic phenomenon? This is a question that will be addressed here with an investigation that remains within the limits of a preliminary essay. In fact, instead of providing a precise and systematic solution, the following essay aims to undertake a survey mapping the various implications that underlie this practice. The latter can be considered exemplary of our current living conditions. This is both because it is connected with the complex problem of aestheticization that has been spreading for several decades in the globalized world, and because it connects the need for a somehow instrumental control of experience, and therefore for its at least partial rationalization, with the equally strong need for flow and apparently immediate familiarity. The combination of the various instances that thus underlie Experience Design, as we shall show, could yield a specific horizon. A horizon in which it is the aesthetic itself that changes its skin compared to the more traditional paradigms usually followed in disciplinary and academic investigations. Also for this reason we deem interesting the idea of adopting the solution of a preliminary essay on the subject, by sampling some instances also about possible references that could then guide further developments of further research.

1.

LAYING THE GROUNDS FOR AN AESTHETICS OF EXPERIENCE DESIGN

1.1. *A Heuristic Horizon of the Aesthetic*

What are we talking about when we talk about aesthetics, and the concept related to it, i.e. "the aesthetic", and also aesthetic experience? Answering these questions is not an easy task. Any definition of them may risk essentialism, and the problem with an essentialist approach to aesthetics and its contents in this specific case is that it fosters rigid, universal "grids". Anything that does not fall within their coordinates can then potentially be dismissed as non-aesthetic. On the contrary, the reality of aesthetic phenomena has always proved itself capable to progressively include within the aesthetic sphere unexpected contents, previously considered irrelevant. One could even say that the history of aesthetic phenomena has belied any attempt to establish an essence of the aesthetic as such, if by the latter we mean the definition of specific, necessary and sufficient characteristics of objects or mental states.

On the other hand, one may say that promoting an anti-essentialist understanding of aesthetics and the aesthetic may end up acquiring the feature of essentialism, as it would in turn prescribe something that should not be pursued nor fostered. We are clearly facing a circularity problem.

Not least, an "anything goes" attitude to aesthetics (but really to anything) and its contents is equally problematic: although we cannot maintain that there are universal laws that can explain certain things, there are somewhat more or less explicitly or implicitly codified rules that at least allow for meaning.

In order to avoid the pitfalls of essentialism, it could be useful for now to put forward a research hypothesis that would allow us to trace a heuristic horizon of the aesthetic which is broad yet meaningful.

At least two anti-essentialist philosophical perspectives can contribute to this process: one is Nelson Goodman's, with his theory of the symptoms of the aesthetic, and the other one has been more recently articulated by Ossi Naukkarinen, who speaks of certain indicators (or issues that are particularly emphasized in specific situations) of the aesthetic. It is not my aim here to discuss them in detail or to take a stance on them, as this would require a work of its own. My aim is rather to employ them, or parts of them, as orienting criteria of the issue at the center of this philosophical essay: the aesthetics of Experience Design. They certainly don't solve the problem, but help frame it. Not only have these two instances of anti-essentialist paradigm or strategy identified what I would call "markers" of the aesthetic, but they have proven a certain efficacy in describing some general phenomena in a productive form.

Goodman maintains what follows:

> [...] I venture the tentative thought that there are five symptoms of the aesthetic: (1) syntactic density, where the finest differences in certain respects constitute a difference between symbols — for example, an ungraduated mercury thermometer as contrasted with an electronic digital-read-out instrument; (2) semantic density, where symbols are provided for things distinguished by the finest differences in certain respects — for example, not only the ungraduated thermometer again but also ordinary English, though it is not syntactically dense; (3) relative repleteness, where comparatively many aspects of a symbol are significant — for example, a single-line drawing of a mountain by Hokusai where every feature of shape, line, thickness, etc. counts, in contrast with perhaps the same line as a chart of daily stockmarket averages, where all that counts is the height of the line above the base; (4) exemplification, where a symbol, whether or not it denotes, symbolizes by serving as a sample of properties it literally or metaphorically possesses; and finally (5) multiple and complex reference, where a symbol performs several integrated and interacting referential functions, some direct and some mediated through other symbols. (Goodman 1978: 252–5)

And Naukkarinen that:

When, for whatever reason, we end up approaching [something] aesthetically, there are typically certain aspects that are emphasized. I believe that they can be clarified by paying attention to four issues: a sense-based approach; the strong role of emotions; a special vocabulary; and a lack of explicit rules of evaluation. These can all be tied together with the concept of taste. I do not believe that we can offer a universally applicable definition of the aesthetic approach through them but they are still frequently mentioned as its indicators. (Naukkarinen 2017)

Goodman's proposal is connoted by a referential, cognitivist and artistic understanding of the aesthetic as something which can be described within a system of symbols. Although his aim was to show that between art, science and ordinary life there is a certain continuity, his "symptoms of the aesthetic" are supposed to answer the question: "*when* is art?".

Naukkarinen's has a more experiential understanding of the aesthetic (between art and non-art), having greater sensibility towards aesthetic phenomena which generally concern human behaviors and practices in everyday environments.[1] He is one of the early proponents of a sub-field of aesthetics named Everyday Aesthetics.

Yet they are intertwined. In Goodman's case, of particular interest is his stressing features such as "density", "repleteness", "complexity", that is, features that would mark the aesthetic as something "opaque", "thick" (on this concept see at least Weitz 1956 and Bonzon 2009, and of course Wittgenstein 1953), hard to unpack or measure as such: a quality, using a Deweyan vocabulary, rather than a quantity.

It is no coincidence that Naukkarinen, in one of the essays (Naukkarinen 2011) in which he lists what he calls "indicators" of the aesthetic, emphasizes also those aspects of Goodman's stance, which allow him to elaborate on and corroborate a fundamental

---

1   For an up to date and systematic treatment of the various topics he has addressed in his very prolific and wide-ranging production see the just published Naukkarinen (2020). This book has appeared just a few weeks before submitting the final draft of my manuscript to the publisher, hence a more extensive analysis of it should be left for another occasion. Yet, Naukkarinen's core concepts addressed here are confirmed also in his latest work.

aspect: the particularity of what is approached aesthetically, or through an aesthetic lens.

This particularity of aesthetically approached things is explained also somewhere else by him (see, at least, Naukkarinen 2013; 2017) precisely by pointing out elements that can be found potentially anywhere in our experience. In these terms nothing is aesthetic as such but in principle anything can become aesthetic. The elements he stresses are the following. 1) The "first-hand", (multi-)sensorial and perceptual dimension of experience: when we experience something aesthetically we experience it directly with our own senses and in situation. 2) The fact that experiencing something aesthetically is emotionally charged: things experienced aesthetically feel good, bad etc., and do not necessarily need to be striking or exceptional as such to be positive, but can involve familiarity and normalcy. 3) The fact that the aesthetic approach to things can also make emerge observations on and evaluations[2] of what has been approached aesthetically. Aesthetic judgments are generally signaled by the usage of a specific (but not necessarily specialistic, at least not in everyday contexts) vocabulary, although the latter is not an "unquestionable proof of them" (i.e. the term "cool", which can generally denote anything positive). Not only, most of the times verbalization is not even involved in them. 4) Finally, how, be them explicit, verbalized, or implicit, perhaps linked to our behaviors and practices, aesthetic characterizations are elastic and dynamically bound to (and can be learned through) use and context: they function well even in the absence of strict or openly codified rules that define them.

What can be derived from these points? That when we deal with the aesthetic we are not dealing with generalizations or quantities, but with particularities that we experience (sense, perceive, feel) as we are personally situated or embedded in qualitatively connoted environments, i.e. (using a sort of technical term) *immersed*[3] in them.

---

2   The peculiar nature of aesthetic judgments has been recently addressed from a phenomenological point of view in terms of a specifically ante-predicative, non-judicative and sub-judicative feature of experience in Matteucci (2019).

3   On the link between the aesthetic and immersivity see Johnson (2018: 247–8). For a critical stance on the concept of immersivity from the standpoint of the philosophical analysis of videogames see Calleja (2011).

1.2. *Experience Design*

How can this heuristic horizon of the aesthetic be related to Experience Design? Of course, in order to answer this question it is necessary to know first what is meant here by Experience Design. Yet, before providing a general description and then a more detailed account of the latter's history, concepts and challenges, it is equally important to delimit the field that we are going to delve into. Suffice it to say for the moment that what's relevant here is understanding in what sense a designed experience can be aesthetic, or in other words, how can Experience Design be a design of aesthetic experiences. Moreover, since design and the aesthetic are addressed here as experiential issues, eventually the point of view that will prevail will be the user's (i.e. the experientor), rather than the designer's.

1.2.1. *General Definition*

We could start from a very basic definition of what in broad terms the label "Experience Design" can denote, such as those that can be found in a dictionary. The label is composed of two words. The first word is "experience", what is done and undergone as an interactive relationship between individuals and environments and/or devices, what can be memorable or emerge as distinctive, and also what can, at some point — gradually, processually — become as integrated as not to be consciously carried out. The second word is "design", the process of management of an even complex function — or, more generally, a complexity — through the intensification and enhancement of already existing, available elements, which are (more or less serially, depending on how exclusive they are aimed at being) made available to "users" or "consumers". It is an intensification of functions, or rather, of their cooperation, by means of unitary and gratifying experiential configurations, which, moreover, even if they are potentially replicable and hence serial, can feel authentic, personal.

Speaking of the design of experiences in these terms, we could potentially mean anything that involves some kind of organization of elements that can afford an experience, a well-flowing experience. Art itself, if considered in its working, could fall into this category.[4]

Yet, basing an inquiry on such a very (and even too) general label, or umbrella term, is not very useful. Instead, we are proposing a conception of Experience Design as a particular configuration of design (typically, and perhaps reductively,[5] meant as an architect's or an engineer's activity) which finds its own historical specification in our contemporaneity, and that *de facto* has not yet sufficiently been approached and thematized from an aesthetic point of view.

We don't want to engage prematurely in an aesthetic discussion, but a couple of examples that are related to it may help us here.

We have mentioned above a relational description of experience, which does not focus either on a "subject" or an "object" as such. The usage of these two terms would imply a dichotomous conception of experience, involving two separate entities. For this reason we previously used (clearly referring to John Dewey's idea of experience as an interaction between "organism" and "milieu") the terms "individuals" and "environments and/or devices". The first one, we believe allows for an understanding of the "experientor" that entails the features of particularity and identity. As for the other two terms implied, we believe that the notion of environment allows locating "individuals" in contexts that are not only natural but also social. These contexts, as far as experience *qua* experience in its operative sense is concerned, imply a scenario (see Peacocke 1992), they are holistic and cannot really be reduced to a single, defined, discrete entity. Or better, one can certainly delimit, frame, and analyze one specific aspect of an environment, but this would concern a theorizing, thematizing level, and not an

---

4   Since even when a work of art is intrinsically antinomic or disharmonious, the resulting aesthetic experience is still that of immersion in its problematic nature: it is all the more successful and effective the more it persists and flows as our own experience.

5   For a thorough "new history" of design putting forward a proposal for its disciplinary emancipation also concerning its actors we refer the reader to Midal (2020). A further, interesting and radical perspective is suggested by Colomina and Wigley (2017), who see design as what specifically distinguishes us as humans. Another way to put the question is understanding design as an attitude, just like Rawsthorn (2018) does, or through the idea of a more general human aesthetic competence that I will address later in this text.

operative one, which is constitutive of experience *qua* experience. Yet, also these "totalities" in which individuals are situated and embedded are particular, qualitatively charged. This also provides an idea of experience which entails both[6] activity and passivity,[7] as the poles involved in it both shape and are shaped by each other.[8] The term "device" is here employed in the most descriptive sense possible. We are not openly embracing the idea of *dispositif* as formulated by Michel Foucault (see Foucault 1977), Gilles Deleuze (see Deleuze 1989) or Giorgio Agamben (see Agamben 2006), for instance, although a thorough analysis of how this notion has been developed in various philosophical traditions would be an interesting project. In our case, "device" means a — real or virtual, concrete or abstract — mediator understood as something able to be conducive to an experience, and to support it during its course. It is not simply a "stimulus" or a "trigger", but it is properly the environment, or medium where it unfolds, where it takes place.

From my point of view, which aims at stressing the relationship or the interaction between the two concepts of organism and environment/and or device according to its aesthetic connotation, such characterization of experience appears fruitful not the least because it allows tracing a distinction between the (aesthetic) experience of artistic or natural elements (following a traditional conception of aesthetics) and the (aesthetic) experience of the everyday. In the first case, being "inside" the (aesthetic) relationship does not rule out the fact that such relationship may be dissonant or even aporetic — as proved by the fact that "somehow positive" aesthetic value has been recognized to works which are particularly complex, or even incomplete, or to natural disasters, for instance. Our experience "of" an artwork can be problematic because of its objective and/or cognitive features (puzzling, dissonant, contradictory, unsettling...) but we are immersed in an aesthetic dimension insofar as our experience "with" it is gratifying (flowing and increasingly involving). In the second case, the gratification

---

6   On the nexus between activity and passivity from a paleoanthropological viewpoint see Malafouris (2013).

7   On the centrality of passivity in aesthetic experience see at least Griffero (2019).

8   Following a pragmatist, phenomenological, and post-phenomenological perspective.

that is immanent in the (aesthetic) experience exclusively concerns relationships between the experientor, or experiencing individual, and the experiential (designed) environment and/or device, in which the degree of facilitation of experiences is maximized. And it cannot be denied that the facilitation, the enhancement (also in terms of the management of problems, between problem solving and problem setting) of experiences is exactly the kernel of (experience) design, where both the experience "of" the device and the experience "with" it are flowing and gratifying (on the distinction between "experience-of" and "experience-with" see Matteucci 2019; 2020)

Of course, with this I am not saying that all everyday experience is designed, or even well-designed, but that everydayness as such concerns an effortless dimension of experience. This is all the more true insofar as a line of research such as Everyday Aesthetics has generally pointed to this dimension in its various investigations, thematizing what has been defined a "tension" between opposing elements such as familiarization–defamiliarization, ordinary–extraordinary, normalcy–strangeness etc., challenging a traditional conception of aesthetic experience. When something happens requiring an effort from our part in order to balance it with and within our current context, this something takes on the character of an extra-ordinary event that "breaks", that interrupts our everydayness. Contrariwise, the characteristic of (experience) design to be emphasized is, more precisely, that it acts as an intensifying factor of the effortless dimension of experience which it aims at making more perspicuous and conspicuous through specific processes. A designed experience device or environment might even in the first place feel unfamiliar or even surprise the user. Yet, it is successful insofar as it achieves its being experienced as fully integrated in the everyday, which is so enriched. It need not escape our ordinary context, making it extra-ordinary, although it may contribute to it something qualitatively new, even something unusual. Thus it works in continuity with everydayness.

Generally speaking, Experience Design concerns experiences that are "artificially" created because they are subjected to construction, valorization and normalization. In particular, but not exclusively, this is so if experiences are meant to be marketed, through procedures that respectively imply a distinction of and an almost ongoing engagement in them; in other terms, experiences that are gratifying, linked to our taste, in their working. We face here a relationship that seems to be inextricable in Experience Design to the extent that it involves gratification, taste and, as a third element, functionality. It does not concern mere instrumentality, since its goals are not external to the usage of a device, and it actually invites our immersion in its field. The gratification that is immanent in such construction, valorization and normalization processes exclusively implies relationships that are aimed at a, and that actually are of utmost, positive facilitation of experience.

Examples of Experience Design can also include certain forms of Critical or also Speculative Design (see Dunne 2005; Dunne and Raby 2013), or those commercial designed experiences such as Escape Rooms. They evidently aim at creating situations in which experiences are not facilitated in terms of their accomplishment but facilitated in terms of providing a "condensed" negative, or at least uncomfortable experience, that would not be experienced otherwise, at least not ordinarily. But these are borderline cases, and we would like to emphasize another aspect, that these designed experiences do not really pursue, nor intensify.

1.2.2. *Processes, Neighborhoods and Identities in the Everyday*

The issue we are concerned with can be explained by stressing how the processuality ascribed to design and Experience Design connotes also someone's everyday. The latter is not "simply" what one experiences daily, or on a daily basis (so "everyday life" should not be equated with "daily life", see Naukkarinen and Vasquez 2017), but a very particular configuration of experience that *emerges from* what philosophy, starting at least from Husserl (1936), has defined as *Lebenswelt*[9] (which hence cannot be equated with "everyday life" either, see Iannilli 2019a: 265–8).[10] The latter, in an extremely basic

---

9   For a study on the origins and reasons underlying this concept in Husserl see Fellmann (1983).

10   In the French academic context we refer the reader to Formis (2010), who discerns the "ordinaire" from the "quotidien". On the one hand, "ordinaire" would be a more general, even transcendental, collective and potential mode of living, while on the other hand "quotidien" would be a dimension with a specific and actual spatiality and temporality which includes the

description, can be defined as a set of practices, ideas, values, etc. more or less shared by various individuals in various contexts. It has the interesting feature of being experienced as original, natural, yet being historical, constituted. Something similar has been elaborated by Bourdieu (1980; 1992; 1997) through the concepts of "habitus" and "field" and their interrelation. His aim was understanding how and to what extent an adjustment is realized between objective structures and structures interiorized by agents in the form of a "practical sense". All of these concepts concern processes which take place in oblique and opaque ways, rather than linear or clear-cut manners. As such, they do not constitute the everyday. They constitute the background from which, so to speak, the everyday emerges. Yet, in doing so, they maintain, at the same time, their operative and hence also opaque connotation.

That is why someone's everyday cannot be reduced to specific objects, people, events, activities, properties, etc. for instance. If anything, it could be defined by the conscious and non-conscious stances, attitudes and relationships we have towards and with them (Naukkarinen 2013). These same stances, attitudes and relationships imply a more or less aware sense of normalcy, habit, safety and identity. Someone's everyday is what stems out of our encounter with what has been elsewhere called "complexual aspect" (Matteucci 2019): it is a scenario as a *pars pro toto* of a "niche" that we inhabit.[11] It inheres in a dimension of familiarity, of contingent stability; in its processuality it can also be re-shaped at various paces by exceptional (positive and negative) elements. It implies a contextual, perceptual, and also imaginative, expectative mode of experience which brings together a dimension of presence, of past and future.[12]

---

various, single applications of this general mode. In other terms, the ordinary would be an invariable, universal dimension of experience while the everyday would be the form, or the set of forms it can take on, variably.

11 This notion has been recently addressed from an aesthetic viewpoint and following different directions for instance by Menary (2014), Portera (2016), Richards (2017), Matteucci (2019). The concept, though, has been formulated originally in evolutionary sciences as a bio-cultural ecological niche in works such as Johnson (1910), Grinnell (1914), Hutchison (1957), Kendal, Tehrani, and Odling-Smee (2011).

12 "One's everyday can be more or less positive or negative, aesthetically or otherwise, but independently of its nature it changes with time. My

In this sense the everyday implies a strong sense of possibility: our (designed) daily life, *Lebenswelt*, field, "complexual aspect", or set of every-day objects, people, events, activities constitute common "neighborhoods" (as they are, for instance, visually rendered in mathematics) that can potentially become "our own", personal (and vice-versa, as we are still talking about processes and mutual relationships). Stressing potentiality justifies also the fact that something, and our relationship towards it, can just be neutral, impersonal, nor positive or negative, and stay that way for us, until it no longer does. Yet, when "neighborhoods" become our own everyday, personal space,[13] our niche, then this dimension is usually positive and is generally what we aim at. However, it can also become frustrating and negative when stagnating and hence we try more or less consciously to escape from it (for a more nuanced explanation of the processuality which connotes the everyday, also through a very helpful visual scheme see Naukkarinen 2013, but see also Melchionne 2013). The same applies to the maximized facilitation of experience provided by Experience Design: while gratifying at first, it may eventually become as frustrating as a poorly designed experience can be. It is a matter of degree in both cases. In this framework the negative experiences afforded by some critical forms of design, or by other commercial experiential forms

---

everyday now is somewhat different from what it was a year ago. This change is partly intentional and controlled, partly not. But it must be emphasized that the change has particularly to do with objects, actions and events, and not that much to do with the everyday attitude that, in the end, constitutes the everyday. [...] However, everydayness remains on the level of the relationship itself: whatever is routine and normal can be a part of our everyday, be that play and toys, fixing a car, or sports. Of course, in some lives the constellation of objects, actions, and events may remain rather stable for long periods of time, but this is not necessary for everydayness to continue.

Although I emphasize the present tense [...], the now of my everyday, it is clear that the past and the future influence all that there now is. I have memories and plans and my past deeds have forged me into what I am. My present experiences are what I now have, continuously and always, but they can be seen as condensed points or prisms of my whole life span, or even of much longer cultural and nature-based processes. The present oozes what there was and what we believe will be" (Naukkarinen 2013).

13   On the relationship between personal space and aesthetics see Lehtinen (2013).

more linked to leisure such as Escape Rooms can be part of what defines our everyday, just like non-designed negative experiences do, while they do not aim at intensifying its core elements that we have described above.

Finally, even if only in passing, it is worth referring the reader here (see Iannilli 2014[14]) to a case in its own way exemplary of the same artificial mixture of experience in relation to design that constitutes the topic of this entire essay. In fact, it could be useful to emphasize the same mixture in relation to a particular case study. The latter concerns the question of the creation of operative interfaces that make everyday places much more than empty spaces. In a technologically structured map, such as those afforded by the various applications we download on our devices and use almost everyday, for instance, the aesthetic dimension filters in such a way as to create neighborhoods of significant density, albeit in modalities that in no way prescind from the technical constraints of the device. Maps and design, in particular, share something that has been defined as "natural mapping" (see Norman 1988: 75–80) in the field of Human Computer Interaction and Interactive Design. It basically consists in a perceptual organization of functions such that an action is carried out in the most natural way possible, in a way the interaction, or the interface as a mediator, does not "feel" extraneous, or a mediator at all. As such, the maps we are talking about are, for the topological paradigm they imply, a valid example of Experience Design.

1.2.3. *Cool Design: Towards a Reconsideration of the Relationship Between Form and Function?*

Experience Design, just like someone's everyday, lies on a threshold between salience and seamlessness. Something is salient when it emerges as significant within a given context,

---

14   This paper was written in the first phases of a research that has led to the topics addressed in this essay. Although it is not totally updated due to the fast developments of the technologies linked to cartography, and although today I would describe some concepts perhaps in a different way and using different and more precise terms, I believe that it still points to some interesting aspects that could help better understand our conception of Experience Design.

and generates some sort of awareness, or draws our attention. Something is seamless when it is not perspicuous or conspicuous as such, as something salient may be, but is rather embedded, smoothly continuous and not consciously carried out.

In these terms Experience Design respectively responds to the problem concerning how to facilitate, afford, or prompt an experience and the problem concerning how to make and keep this process as flowing and immersive as possible, which a designer may make the basis of her/his work. Affording a "happy" (that is, immediate) but not "instantaneous" (that is, mediated) interaction is a fundamental principle in Experience Design. The feature of "happy immediacy" characterizes the experience afforded by Experience Design as positively personal and flowing in the terms described just above. Discerning this feature from "instantaneousness" allows a stress to be made again upon the fact that designed environments and/or devices are not mere triggers, stimuli conducive to experience, but they are also supporting the latter from its emergence and during its course, immersively. Not only, the "not instantaneous", or mediated interaction is such also in the sense it is not something "vertical", sheer or abrupt, so to speak, being instead the result of processes of "horizontal" and collaborative management and organization of already existing materials included in particular situations, or horizons.

Speaking of design processes in this manner is useful for introducing a further friction that design generates within the consolidated system of aesthetics and its actors. In these terms, a designer is no longer necessarily that sort of individual such as the artist who, at least from the 18th century on, was (and still is undeniably) regarded as a unique genius and *ex-nihilo* producer. Contrariwise, the designer[15] does not work "vertically", "demiurgically" so to speak, or according to what we may call a "Promethean"[16] attitude. This conception, of course, may raise

---

15   The "star" phenomenon, or a "genius-like" conception among and of designers is of course a matter of fact. Yet, here we aim at stressing features that emphasize the embedded, material, horizontal, co-operative aspects of design processes.

16   The idea of a "Promethean" kind of productivity is tackled also by Ihde (2010), who speaks of "Promethean-style technofantasies" in his attempt to differentiate a post-phenomenological stance from Heidegger's

the question: "how about innovation in design?". It is not possible to address this topic in detail here, but let me provide a cursory answer by clarifying that although innovation is a fundamental part of design processes, it must be stressed that to "innovate" does not strictly mean to "invent", although an element of novelty is implied in both cases. The nature of this novelty and the abilities of the actors involved in design will be discussed in the second chapter of this essay.

The kind of functionality afforded by Experience Design is a kind of functionality that with good reason could be qualified by the prefix "hyper-". The latter can denote something both in a quantitative and in a qualitative sense. Drawing this distinction can help us define the specific conceptions we are putting forward. Generally speaking, "hyper-" denotes something which is "over", "beyond", exaggerated, extremely intensified as compared to what is deemed "normal". In the first case, that is to say, quantitatively, it concerns something that is excessive, unbalanced, or even unsustainable, and in this sense it can take on a negative connotation. In the second case, that is to say, qualitatively, it concerns an intensification of certain aspects that, as far as certain qualities are concerned, can take on a positive connotation. The same applies to a conception of experience as "hyper-functionalized". Quantitatively, "hyper-functionalization" could be meant as the overwhelming functionalization of every single aspect of experience.[17] Yet, there is an aspect we would like to stress in particular, although it cannot be understood without taking into consideration also the quantitative aspects entailed by "hyper-" experiences and "hyper-" features, which we experience anyways. Qualitatively, it would indicate a level of functionalization of experience that does not require the reference to a function,

---

phenomenological approach to technology. This word choice is aimed at emphasizing the properly interrelational and mutually co-constitutive nature of the relationship between humans and technology which Heidegger, according to him, failed to take into account. For an analysis of the figure of Prometheus from a philosophical-aesthetic point of view see Chiodo (2020).

17   One critical way in which the question of the extreme solution-oriented practice has been addressed is through the concept of "solutionism" (Morozov 2013). Solutionism would refer to the conviction that technology can fix, or solve, any social problem.

to a goal, which are external to experience itself, but that is so intensified as to coincide with the own configuration, with the own form of experience. Something similar has been described from a sociological point of view, for instance, by Lipovetsky (2006) as "hyper-consumption".[18] The latter can be defined as a consumption for "the sake of consumption" that signals a shift from a "possessive individualism" to a "consumeristic, experiential individualism". What counts is not the material possession of something, but the consumption of experiences.

Along similar lines, as far as Experience Design is concerned, form cannot be reduced to the design and usage of a "formed object", of a "forma formata", but rather of a "forma formans"[19] allowing formative, qualitative processes, which can only be implemented indirectly.

Experience Design, as both "designed" and "experienced" could be understood in terms of the pursue of the so-called "self-effacing goals". Although this concept is usually employed in philosophy in order to explain things like moral virtues or the goal of happiness, it is legitimate to make an aesthetic use of it. For instance, Russell (2011) uses it in an attempt to provide a philosophical account of the "effortless cool" person as endowed by a specifically aesthetic competence. "A goal is self-effacing if our achievement of that goal requires that we look away from the goal rather than pursue it directly" (Russell 2011: 47). The concept of coolness is extremely challenging and not easy to unpack, and it is not possible to further address it here (but see Iannilli and Marino 2020). Russell's arguments are elaborate and, in the end, they yield a problematizing account of the effortless cool person, which has many implications. Yet, for the sake of the topic at issue here, we

---

18   This same concept has been addressed aesthetically in Matteucci (2019: 136, 150, 154, 219, 221, 234, 243).

19   The notion of *forma formans* has been central in Ernst Cassirer's work starting at least from his famous project on the philosophy of symbolic forms (1923-29). However, other works focusing on this aspect are also Cassirer (1930; 1931; 1932). The notion of formativity has been central in Italian aesthetics as well, for instance in two diverging perspectives on the topic represented respectively by Luigi Pareyson (1954) and Enzo Paci (1957). The first one was an advocate of hermeneutics as a formative-interpretive process, and the second one of phenomenology as a structural process of experience.

can say that, as far as the latter is analyzed through the lens of self-effacing goals, the philosophical account of the effortless cool person concerns her or his achievement of aesthetic excellence by caring about aesthetic matters in and for themselves independently of what others might think. The more one strives to be, or at least strives to look cool, like no effort whatsoever was made, the less this person is actually going to be cool, or aesthetically competent. It is interesting to note that, going back to Lipovetsky's take on hyper-consumerism, although along different lines, it considers the concept and the phenomenon precisely within the wider issue of a "paradoxical happiness".

How can all this apply to Experience Design? Experience Design is such insofar as there is an organization, a manipulation of "quantities" in order to achieve quality. Yet, the more one strives to obtain quality directly from quantities (i.e. reduces qualities to quantities), the less an aesthetic dimension of Experience Design is at stake.

The conception of Experience Design that I am recommending suggests a need for a reconsideration of the classic couple of form and function, which as we shall see in the next paragraph, has been at the center of design theory and practice since its origins.

1.3. History, Concepts, Challenges

1.3.1. The Practical, the Economic, the Aesthetic

One crucial year in the history of design is 1851, when the first International exhibition, "The Great Exhibition",[20] took place at

---

20 Or at least it is considered to be one relevant factor (either a positive or a negative one) for its development. On the link between The Great Exhibition and the history of design see, among the many, van Wesemael (2001); Bony (2005); Fallan (2010); Vitta (2011; 2012); Mecacci (2012); Margolin (2014); Iannilli (2019a); Midal (2020). Taking a stance on the wider and more complex question of the origins of design broadly understood is not our aim here. Seeing the Great Exhibition as one of the milestones in the history of design, and even 1851 as design's conventional birth year for how we experience it today, is one way to look at the question. There are other accounts that take on a different perspective. One recent example

the Crystal Palace in London.[21] For the first time, objects intended for everyday use in common people's households and produced with industrial procedures were exhibited, mainly for commercial purposes[22], while at the same time claiming the recognition of

---

is the already mentioned Colomina and Wigley (2017), who suggest an archaeological-anthropological understanding of design.

21 Various accounts of the event can be found in Greenhalgh (1988); Hobhouse (2002); Auerbach and Hoffenberg (2008); Young (2009); Bosbach and Davis (2012).

22 On October 13, 1851, an article appeared on "The Times" drafts a review of the event shortly before its conclusion, while also casting a light on its implications and developments, in particular from an economic standpoint: "Of no public event that has ever happened do such complete records exist, From these, speculative minds will hereafter be able to abstract their full significance; but it is now, while curiosity and interest are still awake on the whole subject, and while the closing stimulates these faculties in an unwonted degree, that the full importance is appreciated of giving a practical aim and direction to those vague impressions of wonder which they survey of so many objects leaves behind. Men, in this country at least, do not rest satisfied with sentimental results, and if the doctrines of universal brotherhood and of a new starting point to industry were the only general conclusions that they had to fall back upon, we fear that they might come in a very short time to think lightly enough of the Great Exhibition. *The two great issues raised by the event* [emphasis added] which has just terminated may be briefly stated thus: In what direction as an industrial community should we henceforth travel, and by what means should we proceed? Should we, yielding to those tastes for the splendid, which the possession of great wealth promotes, dedicate our efforts to the costly and the beautiful in production, or should our course be still guided by those unpretending and material influences which have already raised us to such a pitch of prosperity and power? Standing between the civilization of the New World and that of the Old, should we raise our manufactures to the highest European and Oriental standards of taste, or should we still struggle chiefly to extend their boundaries and to command by the element of price, the markets of the world? That is one issue, and is already receiving a solution by which we may hope in time to secure both the alternatives suggested, and to show that, practically, they may be united in the same industrial system. The reports of the juries, the association of such men as Mr. Redgrave, Mr. Cole, Mr. Owen Jones, and Mr. Pugin, for the selection of objects on which to found a pure school of design, the labours of Mr. Digby Wyatt and others in the same direction; and above all, the project of the Society of Arts for the establishment of elementary drawing schools [...] must tend greatly to raise the character of our art manufactures. On the other hand, the mortifying but useful defeats which we have received from our children across the Atlantic, the wide publicity given to new materials, machines and processes, the

their "aesthetic dignity", by presenting also emphasized "formal" features.[23] Such a multifaceted identity of these objects is often difficult to grasp theoretically, being constituted by at least three important elements: the practical, the economic and the aesthetic.

Here we observe the controversial — as it is hard to univocally address and define — nature of design, that is rooted in this occasion and runs throughout the 20th and 21st centuries. It can be described in terms of two poles generally and canonically represented by the concepts of "function" and "form". The former is usually associated with a concrete dimension of usefulness, consumption, and instrumentality and the latter with a more abstract dimension of uselessness, contemplation, and enjoyment. This hybrid nature of design has also generally made it a topic in philosophical aesthetics either long neglected, as not comfortably concerning the traditional "pure" spheres of art or nature aesthetics, or interpreted by using classical aesthetic categories and conceptions belonging to them. Providing an articulated reconstruction of the difficult relationship between design and philosophical aesthetics and the implications for both parts involved is not the aim of this essay (but see Iannilli 2019a). However, suffice it to say that design can be a useful and important testbed and factor for a reconsideration of the disciplinary borders of aesthetics. Furthermore, over the last few years a number of studies addressing the aesthetics of design (yet, not explicitly of Experience Design) have appeared, signaling

---

certainty of an improved patent law in the next session of Parliament, and, above all, the opportunities which [...] have been afforded by the display just terminated for observing how far price affects the prosperity of trade, these and other considerations will keep our manufacturers utilitarian in their character and strengthen vastly the mechanical and inventive genius of the country".

23   This is well summed up by this excerpt from an essay available in the Catalogue of the Great Exhibition: "[In] the following Essay [...] the various species of ornamental art will be examined with respect to their quality, wholly regardless of their magnitude or quantity. [A] great fact displayed, perhaps unavoidable where true education is absent, is the very general mistake that quantity of ornament implies beauty, many objects being so overloaded with details as to utterly destroy the general individuality of expression of the object, and even to render it at first doubtful what the object can be", Wornum (1851: i–ii, vi).

the philosophical relevance of and the challenge represented by such relationship and the conceptual couple connoting it. Some recent monographs can be mentioned: Forsey (2013), who provides a Kantian interpretation of the (everyday) aesthetics of design through the concept of dependent beauty;[24] Folkmann (2013), who takes a post-phenomenological stance on the subject; Parsons (2016), who formulates the notion of "functional beauty"; and Feige (2018), who understands the aesthetics of design between anti-formalism and pluri-functionalism.[25]

The relationship between form and function in its various interpretations is as important in these and other philosophical contributions as it is in design in general since its historical origins. Design has always put a greater or lesser emphasis on one of these poles, and has done it with more or less success. They have in fact often risked being hypostatized, absolutized, on the one hand ending up to the extreme of a technocratic design, and on the other hand of a more hedonistic one.

However, either successful or not, design has always had (and still has) as its fulcrum that of profiling, of shaping experiences, of promoting (even in its extremes, a yet generic) human flourishing.

1.3.2. *The Digital (as a New Phase of Aestheticization)*

In these terms the label "Experience Design" could sound redundant but it is not, since it is a radicalization of this distinctive feature of design in general. Moreover, "Experience Design" could also, but should not, sound oxymoronic. It is true that it is bringing together what is supposed to be intrinsically spontaneous and natural as experience with what is intrinsically artificial as design. Yet, if a processual perspective on experience, and an idea of identity as something that is defined on the threshold of various

---

24 See also Forsey (2015).
25 However, many other philosophical contributions (essays, books, book chapters, entries) on the matter, have also been published. Among them: Flusser (1993); Palmer and Dodson (1996, 2014); Dilworth (2001); Hirdina (2001), Francalanci (2006); Suckow (2006); Griffero (2007); Saito (2007); Kyndrup (2008); Nida-Rümelin and Steinbrenner (2010); Hamilton (2011); De Fusco (2012); Mecacci (2012); Vitta (2012, 2016); Bhatt (2013); Lees-Maffei (2014); Vermaas and Vial (2018); and many others.

elements dialectically interacting is undertaken, the opposition between artificiality and naturality fades. Interestingly, the question of the constitution of identity as a (social) process has been central in fashion studies as well. Emblematical is the debate between essentialist and anti-essentialist theories (for an overview see Edwards 2011), i.e. on the one hand theories (see especially Lurie 1981) that foster an idea of a true/essential self (as absolute, deeply rooted in an alleged "interiority", unique), and on the other hand theories (see Finkelstein 1991; Barnard 1996) that foster (more or less critically) an idea of a constructed/fashioned self (as context-dependent and undecidable, based on appearances, serial and commodified).

However, the first explicit thematization of design as conducive to experience through a related discipline mainly took place during the 1980s and the 1990s, when the development of Human Computer Interaction (HCI) took a specific direction. It is not of secondary importance that digital technologies played an increasingly central role in this process (see Marfia and Matteucci 2018; Manovich 2019; Naukkarinen 2019, who point out how digital technologies have manifold implications for human perception, emotion, everyday life, and aesthetic experience more generally). The digital can hence be viewed as a fourth, important element defining design for how it is experienced today.

The developments occurring during the past four decades signal a very important fact: that a dramatic dematerialization, spreading and embodiment of design in everyday practices has taken place. This process can be described in terms of a shift from designed objects to designed experiences (both in terms of the point of view of a designer and of the point of view of a user[26]). However, the digital and the developments of HCI are not the only relevant elements as far as Experience Design is concerned. Yet, they endow the latter with a historical specification that sheds light on some important aspects. By this, we are not maintaining that it is only with the virtualization–digitalization turn that this shift has effectively happened. Rather, that over these years the

---

26   A further, challenging, way of understanding this process could be from the point of view of AI, meant as something which both designs and is at least partly designed.

ubiquity (global and local) of the experiential component of design — which had already been at least profiled in the previous decades by increasingly popular and mass experiential phenomena — is more evidently accentuated.

It is interesting to note how each of the various passages in which the story of design has unfolded by providing a variable historical specification to the question of the design of experiences can be generally made coincide with the main phases of aestheticization. Aestheticization[27] is understood as a process or a series of processes aimed at giving priority to the aesthetic as compared to the political, religious, ethical (etc.) component of experience while emphasizing aspects usually linked to beauty, pleasure, appearance, sensuality up to the extreme of sensationality (see Türcke 2002). This evolution can be summarized into four main phases of aestheticization. The first phase, during the second half of the 19th century, is the opening of Department stores and International exhibitions that (a) formalize the nexus between aesthetics and economics, (b) develop techniques of *mise en scène* of commodities, and (c) introduce what we may call "proto-design" and "proto-marketing" elements in everyday contexts. The second phase coincides with the first decades of the 20th century, when technology and art, mass production and consumption become increasingly intertwined. The third phase can be identified in the development of pop culture in the 1950s-1960s, whose features are, for example, the impermanence of forms, the power of images in everyday life, the commodification of art, urbanization, and the reduction of cultural hierarchies. The fourth phase is the virtual–digital turn starting in the 1980s-1990s, as mentioned above. During this same period, typically aesthetic categories as taste, pleasure, experience, style, appearance, and creativity become central and predominant in step with the growing importance of media, new technologies and consumption for the definition of both social and individual identities. An important work that

---

27 Recent inquires on the topic are provided by, for instance, Featherstone (1991); Cova and Svanfeldt (1993); Welsch (1996); Böhme (2001); Postrel (2003); Michaud (2003); Nielsen (2005); Naukkarinen (1998, 2012, 2020); Rothenberg (2011); Lipovetsky and Serroy (2013); Reckwitz (2017); Matteucci (2016, 2017); Mecacci (2017).

has pioneeringly grasped the nexus between digitalization and aestheticization is Welsh (1996).

In the first three phases, or stages, some elements start to emerge and progressively become hypertrophic and widespread. In the fourth stage, they, so to speak, really begin to "settle", while it can be said that during own fifth stage in the 21st century, these elements have become even more normalized and infrastructured into the everyday.

1.3.3. *Qualities, Users*

The latter two stages (fourth and fifth) have a particular relevance for the topic at issue here precisely because they bring to the fore the experiential characterization that we deem important. An emphasis on the experiential corresponds to a growing emphasis on the qualitative, and hence the inclusion, in design and HCI discourse, of aesthetic debates. Last but not least, they bring about a focus on the role of the user.

Spence (2016), partly drawing from Bødker (2006), reconstructs what have been defined the "three waves of HCI". The first wave, in the early 1980s "involved many things that were physical and relatively easy to measure", the second wave, in the 1980s-1990s "began to require a way of accounting for context and social interaction" and the third wave "is now pushing the boundaries of what can be effectively conceptualized, much less studied or measured" (Spence 2016: 37).

This is basically the description of the progressive attempts to conceptualize not easily quantifiable elements by assuming a more holistic and environmental approach, and the progressive attempts carried out by designers to define what experience is. (Also, what designers mean by "interaction", while applying empirical means; see Hornbæk, Mottelson, Knibbe, and Vogel 2019).

This passage is important because it is made by one or more disciplines that tend to rely on empirical data and exact measurements, unlike what has been traditionally carried out by a specific aesthetic-philosophical tradition that has made the qualitative dimension of experience in increasingly anthropic and commodified environments its own focal point already between the 19th and the 20th century. The specific qualitative reality of experience has been addressed by often discussing, either with positive or negative tones, a particular notion of experience expressed by the German term *Erlebnis*. This concept has often been used ideologically, treating *Erlebnis* as an experiential mode utterly unlike the external world's, going to the extent of a metaphysical celebration of its ineffability. As such, this conception of *Erlebnis* does not really suit the conception of experience that we are trying to describe here, although today it is still employed for instance in advertising for evocative commercial messages. However, there have been more nuanced and useful manners — also in respect to the topic of this research — of conceiving this notion. They have identified in *Erlebnis* that qualitative dimension of the interaction between the human being and her/his environment, both natural and social, that operatively acts in the same articulation of every other experiential component (discerned as *Erfahrung*). Dilthey (1906) or Simmel (1903), for instance, went in this direction. Dilthey is the advocate of an *Erlebnisästhetik*, in which the notion of experience as correlation is central. Simmel tries to explain the redetermination of the experience of the individual in the metropolitan context — that is, in an environment of "new everydayness" — and starting from the analysis of vital processes (meant as relation *stricto sensu*) aims at providing an adequate justification of the cultural processes of his time. This line of research could also be ascribed to the strategy pursued by Benjamin (1938). By equally dealing with the new experiential dynamics occurred with the metropolitan environment, he opposes what he deems an ideologized and regressive form of experience (*Erlebnis* in its alleged immediacy and irrationality) with the rival notion of *Erfahrung*. The latter, according to Benjamin, affords a more dialectical understanding of experience implying a dialogue, so to speak, a relation. Then, also the phenomenological tradition more generally speaking should be mentioned. By thematizing the concept of *Erlebnis*, phenomenology played a fundamental role in the analysis of experiential structures and dynamics also in respect to the technologization processes of the lifeworld. Avoiding the possible misunderstandings implied by the German terms *Erlebnis* and *Erfahrung*, Dewey (1934) puts forward an understanding of experience as a fundamental relationship between a live creature and an environment. He relieves the concept from a schematically gnoseological characterization while bringing to the fore its dynamic aesthetic-anthropological qualification. More recently, the work carried out by Yves Michaud can be considered a relevant contemporary contribution in theorizing the cruciality of experiences in today's society with a focus on the arts (Michaud 2003), and with a more specific focus on design, that is, on experience design (Michaud 2013).

One of the most extensive and pioneering works in the field of computer sciences that goes in an experiential direction is Wright and McCarthy (2004) who, not coincidentally, largely base their analysis of "technology as experience" on Dewey's (and on Bakhtin's) aesthetics.

Interestingly, Wright and McCarthy also provide a detailed explanation, partly drawing from Kuutti (2001), of how the perception of the role of the user[28] has changed over the last four decades in HCI. That change went from playing the role of a cog in a rational-virtual machine during the 1970s-1980s, to a source of error in the 1980s, and then to a social actor in the 1990s, and finally on being a consumer by the late 1990s and early 2000s.

This path in the history of the user corresponds to a shift of priority in Interaction Design from "pure and simple" Usability to User Experience. User Experience Design, whose founding father can be considered Donald Norman (see Norman 1988), prioritizes the production of a specific kind of interactive experiences. These are experiences in which the importance of a typical feature of Usability (Jordan 1998) as "the ability of a product to provide the functions in an easy and efficient way" (Hassenzahl 2003) is progressively reduced. At the same time, the possibility of affording a more layered kind of experience to a user becomes central. This shift signals a general tendency to overcome a minimalist/ simplicity-oriented, or cognitivist approach to Interaction Design and to emphasize aspects deemed belonging to the aesthetic sphere (such as fun; emotion; delight; performance; identity; style, and so on).

Here, it is necessary to stress one important detail. Although the boundaries between various disciplines and sub-disciplines of design are often blurred, when we speak of User Experience Design

---

28   On this topic see also Margolin (1997).

(that moment in which this important shift starts to become increasingly clear) we are not exactly talking of Experience Design yet.[29] Even only nominally, the elimination of the term "user" from the label does seem to denote something important. It suggests that design now recognizes to the user the acquisition of some sort of responsibility, or ability to respond to something. The user is now perceived as a vector which is integrated in experience itself — hence the idea of a hyper-functionality suggested above — and not as a mere "target" of a designed device.

1.3.4. *Users and Competence*

What is lacking from the reconstruction of the role of the user in HCI is the consideration of its current status in Experience Design. Symmetrically to a hyper-functionality as a distinctive character of the experiential field designed by Experience Design, it could be hypothesized that the user progressively becomes, in turn, the one who must be able to play along, so to speak, with the designed aesthetic field. Sh/e becomes the one who actualizes dynamics inside the experience, not someone who simply enjoys its effects, or that mechanically uses tools. In this sense the user becomes some sort of activator, of "hyper-consumer" — not only a consumer — who finds, in the hyper-functional, hyper-consummatory persistence of her/his own aesthetic field, everyday space, niche, her/his own realization of aesthetic reflectivity, as a reflectivity that remains internal to it. And the properly aesthetic connotation of such an experience seems to consist precisely in this.

From a design point of view, therefore, all this seems to be based on the following assumption. The course of the immersive and interactional experience's arc described above leverages, or rather,

---

29 One of the first contributions that attempted at articulating an "agenda" of Experience Design was still titled "User experience: a research agenda" (see Hassenzahl and Tractinsky 2006). One of the authors of this article, Marc Hassenzahl, later expressed his unsatisfaction for this word choice recognizing how User Experience was a label already charged with specific characterizations which did not fully coincide with his own conception of Experience Design. For a discussion on the topic see https://www.interaction-design.org/literature/book/the-encyclopedia-of-human-computer-interaction-2nd-ed/user-experience-and-experience-design [accessed 20 March 2020].

relies on a tacit and irreducible competence that is presumed to be acquired. And it concerns the particular or contingent, or at the same time personal and situated, or embedded, character of the experience. The type of competence involved in designed experiential practices is not exclusively technological (epistemic) and/or technical (how to apply certain skills), but implies something "more", something that for the moment we will define as aesthetic competence.

The point is that as much as designers design experiences, that is, make certain pre-constituted experiential frameworks available, they can never fully thematize an experience as a whole, but only intensify certain (hence quantitatively) aspects of it, relying on the user's competence to operatively activate and carry out the experiential field (hence qualitatively).

1.4. *Literature Survey*

The literature on Experience Design, i.e. the research that explicitly refers to this specific label, is still at an early stage and sometimes there is no clear-cut distinction between various areas in which the design of experiences is central.[30] The latter include User Experience Design, Experience Design, Experience Marketing (see Schmitt 1999), Experience Economy (see the seminal text by Pine II and Gilmore 1999, and from a sociological viewpoint Schulze 1992) and many other sub-fields of these "experiential" areas of research and study. This is probably due to the interdisciplinary nature of the field, or even to the complexity of the concepts involved in the discourse: not coincidentally, all of these investigations are generally developed around the four distinctive aspects previously ascribed to design: the practical, the economic, the aesthetic and the digital. Here Experience Design is generally described from the point of view of a designer, in terms of a methodology or approach to design, and issues such as a tension

---

30   https://uxdesign.cc/experience-design-a-new-discipline-e62db76d5ed1;
      https://www.interaction-design.org/literature/book/the-encyclopedia-
      of-human-computer-interaction-2nd-ed/user-experience-and-
      experience-design [accessed 20 March 2020].

between the qualitative and the quantitative, immediacy and mediation, ongoing engagement and disengagement, a personal level and a ubiquitous level, problem solving and problem setting often recur.

Indications and suggestions on the topic are available on specialized websites,[31] and on a number of essays, book chapters, entries or edited volumes such as Blythe et al. (2009); Forlizzi (2010); Benz (2015); Poldma (2016); Matté Ganet (2017). Yet, only a few monographs have extensively addressed an "Experience Design" until now, and each of them has a very distinctive take on the subject.

For this reason it seems worth it providing an overview of them. This overview does not aim to be exhaustive. There are certainly other volumes which although not openly using the formula "Experience Design" anyway deal with the relationship between design and experiences. Since this is an initial contribution aiming at understanding better a historical specification of design as an Experience Design and some of its implications for aesthetic experiences, though, it seems useful to start precisely from those works which have tried to somehow "institutionalize" it. In doing so, a reconstruction of the aesthetics implied by these contributions will also be provided.

1.4.1. *Hassenzahl*

Among the contributions on Experience Design, Hassenzahl (2010) focuses on interactive products and narrativity.

> [...] The notion of 'scripting' an experience, of creating a narrative of acting through a product [...] are central. Before determining the functionality of a product (the 'what'-level) and ways to operate this functionality (the 'how'-level), the experience designer creates the story of product use. [...] To develop [...] enhanced narratives is crucial to Experience Design. (Hassenzahl 2010: 70)

---

31 See https://www.foolproof.co.uk/journal/experience-design-a-definition; https://medium.theuxblog.com/the-5e-experience-design-model-7852324d46c [accessed 20 March 2020].

The development of such enhanced narratives stems out of the specific approach to design that Hassenzahl defines as his own: an experiential, need-based approach, that is to say, concerning "the 'why'-level".

> The fulfillment of psychological needs is important to every healthy human being. However, depending on the situation at hand, the urge felt to fulfill needs may vary. This urge arises from need deprivation — repeated or prolonged episodes in which need fulfillment is blocked. To identify those blocks is an important starting point for Experience Design. It is difficult to 'sell' an experience of a certain type to somebody who is already highly saturated. However, the true challenge for Experience Design is to fulfill needs without making this too obvious. (Hassenzahl 2010: 58)

This psychologically informed approach also explains the three (good) reasons why, according to Hassenzahl, experience should be considered a design objective (chapter 2). Experiences shape our identity (they have a "self-defining nature"), they increase our well-being (they have the power to "make us happier"), and by fulfilling certain needs they can make us engage in certain activities (they become "a source for motivation").

Hassenzahl programmatically distinguishes the concept of "an experience" from "experiencing" (although without an explicit reference to John Dewey, who notoriously based his theory of experience also on this distinction). He describes the latter, on the one hand, as "a continuous stream emerging from perceiving, acting, thinking, and feeling" (Hassenzahl 2010: 19). An experience, on the other hand is

> an episode, a chunk of time that one went through — with sights and sounds, feelings and thoughts, motives and actions; they are closely knitted together, stored in memory, labeled, relived and communicated to others. An experience is a story, emerging from the dialogue of a person with her or his world through action. (Hassenzahl 2010: 8)

The feature of emergence (or "uniqueness"), though, does not prevent Hassenzahl from defining experiences from a design perspective as "emergent, yet shapeable", basing this fundamental principle on the assumption that the many commonalities of experience can be reduced to properties and patterns, and hence designed.

He lists in chapter 2 of his book "crucial properties of experience". An experience is subjective: "it emerges through situations, objects, people, their interrelationships, and their relationship to the experientor" (Hassenzahl 2010: 9); it is holistic: "it will never focus on a small proportion of processes and aspects only" (Hassenzahl 2010: 27); it is situated: "it will never be context-free"; dynamic: it is "extended over time"; and it is positive.

When addressing this last point Hassenzahl links it to "deliberately designed experience". This means that not deliberately designed experiences (such as being mugged) can be negative while having all the other attributes (i.e. properties) of an experience, but when it comes to Experience Design experiences must be "'worthwhile' or 'valuable' [...] because they [must] fulfil universal psychological needs".[32] However, according to Hassenzahl this does not imply that in Experience Design negative experiences should be dismissed altogether, unless they do not "allow for a higher, valuable end" (Hassenzahl 2010: 32).

In this volume Hassenzahl does not either extensively or explicitly address the role of aesthetics in Experience Design. Yet, he proposes a so-called "pragmatic/hedonic" model that he had already widely developed in some of his previous works. Here he basically addresses two fundamental qualities implied in the interaction with a product: the first one signals the (perceived) ability of a product to accomplish "do-goals" (in which the focus is on its instrumentality), the second one signals the (perceived) ability of a product to accomplish "be-goals" (in which the focus is on the Self). Although conceived of from a psychological viewpoint, this model somehow implies aspects that Hassenzahl himself traces back to the aesthetic sphere in Hassenzahl (2008). Here he openly investigates the question of the aesthetics of interactive product design due to a lack of interest in the topic in HCI. He enucleates three possible approaches in HCI

---

32   In stressing this, he emphasizes the importance of a shift in psychology from "a science of healing" (Hassenzahl 2010: 28) to a science that emphasizes fulfilment, a positive psychology. An instance of an aesthetic account of a positive psychology approach can be found in Melchionne (2014; 2017).

to aesthetics, which he basically equates with beauty: a normative approach, an experiential approach, and a judgmental approach. While providing general indications on the first two, in the course of the contribution he then focuses only on the third. He describes this approach as interested in "the consistency" and the rapidity and easiness of judgments of beauty among individuals, and in the relationship of beauty with other attributes of a product such as novelty and usability. It is not possible to offer here a broader reconstruction of the contents of this text by Hassenzahl but suffice it to say that his contribution consists of an attempt to facilitate the process of integration of beauty concerns in HCI by clarifying certain crucial aspects. The latter involve, for instance, focusing on beauty judgments in terms of the evaluation of the visual Gestalt of a product; recognizing beauty as primarily hedonic "i.e. more concerned with self-referential goals ('be') than action goals ('do')". This point is of particular interest here as it seems to provide more indications on the author's conception of the aesthetic. Hassenzahl describes beauty as a more "readily accessible" and "easy to observe" attribute (which, according to him, is usually perceived in the first place and as relatively stable) as compared to usability. Anyhow, from a holistic viewpoint, he also allows that it is not easy to distinguish these aspects unequivocally, thus recognizing how much the importance of judgments of taste depend on what is emphasized in a specific context, beauty or task performance, for instance.

It is important to note that although Hassenzahl stresses certain aspects and neglects some other aspects, he does recognize the complexity that derives from taking into consideration also aspects that he deems belonging to the aesthetic dimension. In this sense he sees the project of integration of beauty in an empirically driven user-centered design as both a goal and a challenge for HCI.

1.4.2. *Newbery and Farnham*

A second important contribution in the currently available literature on Experience Design is that by Newbery and Farnham (2013), who work at the intersection of business and design. Their focus is on value, that they look at through a specific lens: Experience Design. Experience Design, according to them, "is about solving the problems of creating and identifying value for customers and creating a coherent experience across the entire interface between the business and its customers".[33] For Newbery and Farnham there is a great difference between the "techniques for delivering value" (the "how"), and value itself (the "why"), which should be Experience Design's priority. Experience Design, for them, "is in no way a science or [...] a predictive tool [but the analogy applies] of experience design as the calculus for businesses to use in building engagement around value for their brand and customers". Their proposal revolves around this openly cognitivist conception of experience which stresses the features of temporality, meaningfulness, expectation, and the link between consciousness and unconsciousness:

> [Experiencing] is a basic process, an action that is a fundamental part of the human existence: the use of information that you have received through various means to form an opinion about what the world outside of you is about and how things there are likely to work. Each experience is the set of information you have noticed and stored, along with your emotional and rational responses that arose from the process of receiving the information and making sense of it at the moment of occurrence, modified through the reinforcement or weakening of these perceptions based on other experiences that have accumulated over time. [...] Much of this occurs in ways that are largely outside of our conscious focus. We aren't always aware that we are learning, but what we learn affects our thinking.

Newbery's and Farnham's book is articulated into three main parts. The first one offers a more theoretical and contextualizing analysis of the phenomenon at issue, while the other two parts provide a more concrete contribution aimed at offering exemplifications.

We will mainly deal here with some aspects of the first part precisely because it provides useful indications on the main concepts addressed: design, business, change and Experience Design.

Newbery and Farnham also provide historical remarks on the relationship between business and design (oscillating

---

33 All the excerpts from Newbery and Farnham (2013) are quoted from the ebook, where no exact page numbering was available.

between integrations and divergences): from an evolutionary-anthropological account of design, the distinction between technology and design and the relationship (and split) between maker and designer, the Arts and Crafts movement, the International Style, the origins of the modern brand, etc., to the development of computing and network technologies between the 20th and the 21st century.

We will focus here on a new phase of the relationship between design and business (due to the increasing digitalization of experience) that the authors analyze, since it both sheds light on our situation in the present age and radicalizes certain aspects which are central for Newbery's and Farnham's take on Experience Design: the question of time and value, understood between designing, or operating, and experiencing in rapidly evolving contexts and keeping the customer's engagement ongoing.

Newbery and Farnham stress a double, very important feature of design: it can be understood as both a noun and a verb. It concerns both a "product", or outcome, and processes. One of the goals of their project is to "help bridge the gap between the process and the outcome sides, and create more value for [...] clients". This gap is generally due to the fact that processes (and all their implications) stand on the side of the producer, while the one dealing with the outcome of these processes, i.e. with the "product" (even if what is designed is a service), is the customer, who has a first-hand (that is, immediate, although largely mediated, we may say) experience with the latter.

This distinction is not of secondary importance, in particular if "brand experience" is introduced in the equation, as these authors suggest to do. It qualifies the type of value that they seek to promote: "[the] value delivered by a service is different from that delivered by a product. A service requires an ongoing perception of values by the customer, or the customer stops paying for it, unlike a product, which is purchased once".

It is not coincidental that Newbery and Farnham define themselves as designers active more on the strategy's side, rather than on the product's side. Moreover, rather than making reference to users, they tend to refer to customers, and this is quite understandable, given their openly business-oriented approach. They stress the importance to intensify the collaboration between business and design as such, but also to develop and manage experiential dynamics which are both top-down, such as those carried out by a "CEO", a "chief *experience* officer" and bottom-up, by taking into account the experience, expectations and needs of their customers. In this sense, a part of their strategy is to distinguish between at least three types of value: tangible (measurable and objective), intangible, aspirational (hard to measure and subjective).

> One of the possibilities arising from creating and competing on intangible and aspirational value is a disparity between what value is offered and what value is received. Although this is true for tangible value as well, it's a little easier to spot the discrepancy before committing to the purchase. It's not difficult to see that the more intangible and aspirational value is involved, the more subjective this evaluation can be.

As I said, an important, new phase of the collaboration between business and design was determined, between the 20th and the 21st century, by the "development of computing and network technologies", while services started to be "productized by software" and new fields of design emerged as interface and interaction design. In this context, the relationship between process and outcome was altered, according to Newbery and Farnham, in particular as time gained an increasingly important role. The technological contexts in which business and design were operating and in which customers were experiencing, started to rapidly evolve. This accelerated context radicalized aspects such as value perception, and hence the challenge of keeping an ongoing engagement of the customer. The following quotation is quite exemplificative:

> a modern business has many moving parts. But from a customer's perspective, what they see are facets of a single thing: an interface that connects them to the business, [...] and through which value is represented and ostensibly flows. [...] Business relies on design to help create these interfaces.

Yet, for Newbery and Farnham, Experience Design does not concern the mere usability of interfaces or just problem solving as if it were customer service design. Rather, it strategically "addresses the totality of all the elements of the business, brand and customer".

At the same time, brand is not simply branding, which Newbery and Farnham describe as generally pertaining to the level of discursive or visual expressivity. These distinctions are necessary in order to stress again that Experience Design is value-focused, i.e. it places an emphasis not only on the "how" (pertaining to the techniques for delivering value) but also on the "why" (pertaining to value itself).

Discerning the "how" level from the "why" level is also important as it provides some hints on their conception of aesthetics. The latter does not play a central role in their strategy, as it belongs to the "implementation level".

> There is no question that behavior, aesthetics, materials, human response, and craftsmanship are all important. They are, after all, the components from which experiences are made. But we think that our approach to experience keeps the discussion of these aspects of design at the implementation level — the how of delivering value, not the why.

In this sense Newbery and Farnham also criticize Pine II and Gilmore (1999). Although they also stress the importance of a shift from products to services in their seminal work on Experience Economy, they emphasize the "how" or the "delightful" aspect of experience, which for Newbery and Farnham is not core value — that is to say the "why" — which would actually provide a long-lasting engagement.

1.4.3. *Wendt*

The contribution offered by Wendt (2015) is the most philosophical one among the books on Experience Design here analyzed. As its evocative title "Dasein for Design" clearly suggests, his approach is specifically phenomenological, since "Dasein" ["Being there"] is one of the core concepts of the philosophy of Heidegger, one of the founding fathers of phenomenology.

A good starting point to address Wendt's thorough contribution is the opposition between "development", as something done in a "vacuum space", and "design" as something concerned with context and users.

> So far, we've done an excellent job of developing products, but a terrible job of *designing* products. That is, we've swung the pendulum too far from 'thinking' to 'making', which is resulting in masses of products lacking utility or potential for meaningful interaction. [...] Startup economies and venture capital firms have emphasized speed to market and returns on investment, to the point where 'the launch' has become a fetishized event. Products are 'designed' in a matter of weeks, even days. They are isolated from the entire product's landscape and designed in a vacuum. [...] While this is not to say design should be a long drawn-out process, it certainly should not be an afterthought. We need to take the time to understand the nature of problems and user needs, the implications of our design decisions, and how design executions manifest themselves in the world. (Wendt 2015: 8–9)

This distinction reflects the same distance that Wendt identifies between industry and academia. The former emphasizes the centrality of customers', or end users' insights, yet basically applies biased methods which contradict that accentuation, whereas the latter is generally perceived as too theoretical and hence detached from necessary design practice.

Wendt identifies the root of this dichotomy in a paradox which is typically at stake as far as design is concerned: the "problem-solution paradox".

> What I like to call the problem-solution paradox states that we cannot think about solutions until we understand the problem, and we cannot understand a problem until we think about solutions. (Wendt 2015: 73)

This paradox makes the core of Wendt's investigation, and for this reason we will mainly deal with it here. As mentioned, phenomenology, and in particular Heidegger's philosophy of technology is the lens through which he addresses the question of Experience Design. Yet, he does so not ideologically but by productively comparing and integrating it with its developments and overcomings advocated by such post-phenomenologists as Don Ihde and Peter Verbeek in the direction of a material and interrelational account of the human-technology relationship. In this sense, the "problem-solution paradox"[34] is also at the basis of this transition[35] from phenomenology to post-phenomenology, insofar as, by stressing the role of embodiment and of technology as a mediator in the human-technology relationship, it implies "new ways of concerning ourselves [as designers] with end users and the empathetic process of understanding" (Wendt 2015: 71).

By aiming at avoiding the shortcomings of a rigidly binary, causal and linear understanding of design, Wendt's proposal for a phenomenological and abductive design thinking concerns the need to treat Experience Design in all its complexity, while also being aware of the intrinsically fickle nature of the phenomenon. This involves a reconception of the ways one thinks of problems and solutions. They should not concern the pursue of schematic distinctions and false assumptions on "starting points", but rather a stress on the ways *how* problems and solutions manifest themselves within a context.

The paradoxical character, or complexity of design, and in particular of Experience Design, is something that informs Wendt's book as a whole. He asks a crucial question: "is it really possible to design experiences?". This is explained, for instance, when he treats the issue of the "rift" (also following Mitcham 2001) between producers and users which occurs in design meant as a specifically modern thing, namely, as a post-craft-based society thing, where the one who creates something is not the same person who uses it.

> The interaction designer must assert some kind of control over the use of the object, usually through things like strong information architecture, explicit affordances, and clear instruction. But all of these things have to do with specific elements of the interface,

---

34 He also stresses how this paradox has also been central in anti-dualistic philosophies. Wendt's examples are Rittel and Webber (1973), Dorst (2006), Heidegger's hermeneutic circle and de Saussure's chain of signification, among the many.

35 For a detailed account of this shift, see chapter 5 of Wendt's book "Phenomenology to Post-Phenomenology to Object Studies".

not necessarily the experience. [...] This point is crucial to understanding experience design. There is a key difference between a product or service, and the experience of that product or service. Surely, we cannot dictate the experience, as it is a purely personal phenomenon. Experience is based on unique interpretation and is often vastly different across individuals. But while we might not be able to dictate experience, we can certainly design for the potential of certain qualitative experiences over others. (Wendt 2015: 12–3)

This allows Wendt to provide both a definition of Experience Design and a description of the type of activity carried out by an experience designer.

Experience design is an inherently fickle endeavor; our inability to create causal relationships between users and their designed environments forces us to take a broad view of experience design — understanding it as the emergent effects of many design practices, rather than a practice in itself. An experience designer might design interactions, objects, interfaces, services, products, none of these, or all of these. What emerges out of their interactions with one another, and with a user, is an experience. The design of experiences, then, is an inherently multi-disciplinary and trans-disciplinary practice, involving fields of expertise from both inside and outside of design. (Wendt 2015: 13)

Wendt's goal is to foster an understanding of design theory and practice as something not over simplistically linear but by precisely making the paradox moot, that is to say by making design practice itself a wicked problem emphasizing complexity and focusing on totalities, rather than on "isolated solutions to discrete problems" (Basalla 1988).

By hence suggesting to understand paradoxes as antinomies (like we do here, even more explicitly with the treatment of Adorno's stance, as we will see in the third chapter of this essay) he states that:

They are not to be solved, or perhaps are not even solvable. They are contradictions that must be. If the state of design sways too far to one side, we end up with an ecosystem of products and services that fail to recognize design's inherent complexity. To take even

one of these antinomies and define one of the poles, the results are
disappointing. [...] That is, we cannot necessarily pick an optimal
spot in the space between their poles, as that point is always shifting
depending on the context. What these antinomies point out is the
fundamental complexity of design, which designers often attempt to
push away in lieu of focusing on individual practices. [...] Exploring
this complexity is the key goal of phenomenological design thinking.
(Wendt 2015: 82–3)

This also allows Wendt to stress another paradox which actually
provides his brief aesthetic account of Experience Design. This
paradox has to do with the relationship between what's tangible
and what's intangible, and the ability to evoke meaning, to stress
potentiality. If experiences as such cannot be designed but the
mediation of something is always necessary, then designers must
take into account both material aspects and immaterial qualities
of objects, both their "conscious interpretation" and "unconscious
experience". In this way, according to Wendt, Experience Design
also entails a "challenged aesthetics", insofar as the aesthetic is
defined, following Folkmann (2013: 63) as "the overall process of
the distribution of meaning by means of aestheticization — both
by a sensual staging of experience and by shaping the discursive
and informational setting of knowledge and meaning".

1.4.4. *Spence*

The fourth and final author examined in this survey is Spence
(2016), who speaks of a "Performative Experience Design" (PED).
The latter lies in an area between Performance Studies and
Experience Design, although Spence carefully endows it with its
own specific characterization as PED. As a result, Spence's book is
a very articulated contribution as it addresses the latter from the
points of view of both its "twin lineages". However, in this context
we will focus exclusively on those aspects that clarify the general
project of a PED and its relationship with Experience Design. PED is
a borderline case of Experience Design as it tends to emphasize the
generally salient, uncomfortable aspects of designed interactions.
Among the four monographs analyzed so far, this is the one
that more openly provides an aesthetic account of the design of

experiences, an account of its "how". Spence makes a very precise use of aesthetics understood as an artistic and aesthetic modality concerned with human interactions that take place over time, that is to say as performance.

She locates her research in that third wave of HCI, which is interested in dealing with things that cannot be easily thematized or measured, encompassing aspects such as "affect", "fun", "enchantment", and "aesthetics". In doing so, Spence's PED also fundamentally pursues the goal of generating awareness on specific issues and transforming the experiencing subject.

In other terms, PED fosters aesthetically designed interactions for ethical purposes, which generally concern our (potentially harmful) relationships with technology, which today is all the more shaping our perception of the self, of the other and of the world: our identities.

> PED challenges emerging digital practices, not necessarily because the designer has decided that they are bad, but because there is value in questioning assumptions that are helping to shape our sense of self in the world. (Spence 2016: 15)

PED's technological products are not mass produced nor consumed, but rather aim to gently generate discomfort and reflectivity. In this sense they are not "simply used", but they are to be "dwelled with", also signaling the importance of a shift in design from problem solving towards problem setting.

As I said, PED draws from both Experience Design and Performance Studies which according to Spence both share an interest in performativity and performance, with a focus on technology.

> Performative Experience Design (PED) [is] a methodology, a field, and a framework for understanding interactions with technology in which the device, system, or situation creates an opportunity for the 'user' to perform for others. Performance is not limited to the professional acting of roles on a stage, but the conscious display of behaviour that others might observe. In other words, PED directs our attention away from a technological device or even the user's interaction with that device, towards the powerful internal and interpersonal shifts in perception that are brought about by

displaying our interactions with technology and *appearing* to others as beings engaged with others through technology. (Spence 2016: 2)

What emerges here is also a "public", shared, "dialogical" (shifting between a "I" and a "we") dimension of PED in which there is a conscious, first-hand involvement of subjects appearing and appealing to others' sensibility as engaged. What is mostly of interest for us here is how this relates to the field of Experience Design:

> PED is an extension of experience design. It pushes experience design in the direction set out [...] to explore the most nebulous elements of experience with as much rigour as the pioneers of HCI studied the speed of pointing at an on-screen target. But rather than attempting this exploration with the incredibly wide-ranging concept of 'aesthetics', it uses the aesthetic or artistic mode that directly addresses engagements between people over time: performance. (Spence 2016: 39)

Addressing the question from this point of view is particularly interesting precisely because it makes emerge the importance of aesthetics in PED and, more generally, within the tension between qualitative methods and positivist attempts to derive models of experience that connotes the discourse on designed interactions.

> The entire premise of PED rests on [the observation that experiences are not data] and the conclusion that can be drawn from it, namely that experiences cannot be transmitted as objects or data can, but must rather be 'occasion[ed]' in others, a process through which new experiences are generated. [...] PED uses digital technology to 'occasion' new experiences that cause 'organisms' to view their 'environments' — including the digital aspects of those environments — in a different light. (Spence 2016: 39)

Here Spence is clearly using a Deweyan paradigm, which puts forward an environmental, holistic, processual and transformative idea of aesthetic experience as a heightened experience. Quite interestingly, this seems to testify to a very important fact. Although Spence's viewpoint and role is the first-person perspective of a designer (which also conflates with the first-person perspective of a performer) who is trying to understand the "how" of people's interactions in order to design them, she recognizes that this "how" can only be occasioned, or "nudged", or even intensified, as experiences take shape in processual, interactive manners. They do not merely have to do with "products as experienced".

Moreover, she interestingly states that:

> Aesthetic experiences have the potential to tap precisely the types of non-task-oriented, emotional, affective, and interpersonal realms that third-wave HCI tries to investigate. I argue that any framework of experience design or user experience that fails to account for the aesthetic in this sense is incomplete. (Spence 2016: 40)

So, the aesthetic has a central role in the whole performative-technological, or "intermedial", framework that Spence analyzes. A further way she has to corroborate this importance is by combining, or rather integrating, Erika Fischer-Lichte's discussion on the aesthetics of performance with Ellen Dissanayake's idea of "making special".

The first author (see for instance Fischer-Lichte 2008) encompasses concepts such as heightened attention (towards objects, people and structure of the performance event), the collapse of dichotomies (i.e. between ethics and aesthetics), autopoiesis and emergence (i.e. the event self-generates itself), liminality and transformation (i.e. through and in a performance event, the audience may enter a liminal state in which "emotions, attitudes and behaviours" are transformed). Dissanayake, for her part, clarifies what distinguishes the "extraordinary", or "the aesthetic" in terms of a "making special". This notion refers to the appeal made to someone else's capacity to appreciate "a specialness that is more than what is necessary to fulfill a practical end" (see Dissanayake 2003: 28). It is the outcome of a process of transformation of the "encrusted aspects" (or at least potentially encrusting) of the everyday that PED aims at carrying out, too.

> One way of understanding PED is as a way for people to make our everyday lives 'special' (Dissanayake 2003), including those elements of digital technology that have become embedded in our routines, by heightening attention to the elements of interaction and therefore creating opportunities for liminality and transformation. (Spence 2016: 59)

1.5. *Implications: Towards a Reconsideration of the Relationship Between Form and Function*

We can sum up the main points previously emerged as follows, that is to say, by emphasizing how Experience Design generally implies the notion of threshold, of liminality, of continuity, rather than dichotomies. We believe that it is precisely this "shifting" — or antinomic, we may say — nature of design that makes it a challenging topic.

As far as Experience Design is concerned, we are dealing with:

- an openly experiential turn (i.e. from objects as such to experiences, or rather, from discrete, definite entities to dense, immersive totalities) in design research and in design consumption. In the first case what is implied is a shift from a mainly quantitative to a qualitative approach; from a mainly cognitivist to an aesthetic approach; a focus on the role of the user not in terms of a "target" but in terms of a vector which is completely integrated into and necessary for the configuration of the experiential field. In the second case what is implied is a general tendency to value the overall elements revolving around a certain experience, rather than the mere material possession of something;

- an idea of engagement in experience between salience, or some sort of awareness and attention and seamlessness, or some sort of unaware, flowing immersion. If viewed from the perspective of the designer this dialectical, ever-shifting relationship can be understood as concerning what can be defined as problem setting and problem solving. These two concepts can be meant, respectively, as the generation of points of relevance in the flow of experience and the "silent", "nudge-like" functionalization of experience. This shifting relationship can be understood, also from the point of view of the user, as the pursue of self-effacing goals;

- an emphasis on processes that implies a dismissal of the opposition between natural and artificial, and an anti-essentialist idea of identity;

- an understanding of the relationship between form and function which implies a "hyper-functionality", that is, a functionality that coincides with the configuration of experience itself (in a processual and environmental sense), with the "form" of the experiential field as such; it concerns the creation of a personal, everyday space, a niche that works;

- an idea of competence which, when aesthetic, is not necessarily technological or technical;

- the pre-constitution of an experiential framework, which can be seen either positively or negatively. It is negative when one sees in it a generic pre-determination of the behaviors of the aesthetic user or consumer, in which, again, the "user" would be an unreflective, acritical target or a "spectator" for whom a designed device is only instrumental. Such ubiquitous facilitation of experience in everyday life, in this merely instrumental sense, can lead to a certain lack of experience resulting in alienation — if too "delegated" — and/or inconsiderate hedonism — if "abused" —, and hence be unsustainable, both for individuals and for environments (i.e. ubiquitous as generic, measurable). On the other hand, this same ubiquitous facilitation of experience through the design of pre-constituted experiential frameworks can be seen positively when the experience with the environment and/or device becomes an experience of intensification of one's own experiential field, one's own identity, one's own reflectivity. In this case it can also have an emancipatory potential in its being "hyper-consummatory" and gratifying (i.e. ubiquitous as overarching and particular, non-measurable). It is no longer instrumental, but "useful" in a richer way.

This duplicity might be due to the fact that in Experience Design, paradoxically, although experience refrains from being fully, completely thematized, it is nevertheless something that is still to be designed, that is, intensified, enhanced. A successful Experience Design, then, is not thematizing as such, it is not prescriptive, but intensifying, "inviting": it implies the manipulation of the quantitative in order to obtain quality.

By this, though, it should not be inferred that the aesthetic, in its being "untamable" is also "ineffable"; the point that we aim to stress is that it is rather irreducible to a set of specific properties, but as I said at the beginning of this essay, is signaled by certain markers, or indicators of its presence.

In turn, by this, it should not be inferred that design's role is merely to "nudge" (see Thaler and Sunstein 2008) experiences, as its role for the enhancement of the quality of life is fundamental. Yet, stressing this aspect allows to make emerge the fundamental human and humane component of designed experiences which is usually deemed to disappear when design becomes so pervasive.

However, while addressing these features of Experience Design some issues were only raised in passing or introduced as heuristic hypotheses, and they actually deserve more attention. They basically concern the following questions:

- If the human and humane component is necessary for the accomplishment of a "good" Experience Design, what kind of user's competence is at stake here?
- Is there room for creativity and sustainability in a radically designed environment? And, if so, how can this sustainability be also gratifying?
- How does the anti-essentialist heuristic horizon of the aesthetic with its features of "density" and "quality" fit this designed experience dimension?

We will try to answer these questions by going back to two perspectives on form and function provided by the contributions of two philosophers with great diagnostic and prognostic abilities: John Dewey and Theodor W. Adorno. Overall, they lived all the stages of aestheticization (or at least some of their implications) that led to the configuration of Experience Design as we experience it today, although not in its digital, widespread and normalized phase, for biographical reasons (Dewey was born in 1859 and died in 1952 while Adorno was born in 1903 and died in 1969). They have dealt with their contemporary reality in terms of taking into account what we may define as "objective conditions" and "the primacy of the object", which in the context of the present investigation could be also redescribed as the widespread design of experiences. Specifically, we will address two works in which these philosophers put aesthetics and the aesthetic at the center of their inquiry. Not only: they both deal with them by proposing an anti-essentialist treatment of the relationship between form and function. By doing this, we also aim to shed a novel light on, or at least to provide a more nuanced account of their specific stances and, perhaps, to combine them: on the one hand John Dewey's optimism seeing Experience Design as emancipatory and democratic, and on the other hand Adorno's (alleged) pessimism seeing Experience Design as alienating. Hopefully, then, also the examination of some core concepts of Dewey's and Adorno's philosophical programs — which we deem extremely topical and relevant still today — will make appear as further justified the choice to take as examples, in the introduction, that recent fashion show and advertisement.

1.6. *A Farewell*

Before continuing with the analysis of Dewey and Adorno, we believe it is useful to draw some conclusions here on other aspects that so far have helped to delimit the framework of our analysis. A number of times reference has been made to the fact that an anti-essentialist perspective implies a reconsideration of the traditional boundaries and categories of aesthetics. This has entailed a bringing to the fore of the relevance of everyday experience in particular *as* designed. We have also referred to the philosophical perspective known as Everyday Aesthetics, for it is one of the most recent exemplary attempts to define a useful notion of aesthetic experience free from some cultural debts to the modern philosophical tradition.

However, Everyday Aesthetics as a line of research that has evolved in recent decades does not seem entirely satisfactory for investigating some implications of its own research program, which it generally either tends to neglect or tends to address from a point of view that is ethical-ecological, rather than specifically aesthetic. This is the case at least *insofar as* the issue of aestheticization coupled also with that of digitalization (and therefore also of technologization) is concerned. As we have seen, this is an important coupling which has been quite evidently implied by the treatment of Experience Design that has been carried out so far in this essay. Indeed, we believe that the wider nexus design–everyday–experience should not be overlooked since as such it offers qualifying moments — that are relevant not least — for contemporary aesthetics. This remark can be synthetically explained through the following transitions. First, design became an urgent topic when the opposition between (art- and nature-centered) aesthetics and the everyday was perceived as particularly evident. Second, as we shall see, Everyday Aesthetics took shape when an attempt was made to identify, by opposite reaction, aesthetics with the everyday. Third, the topic of experience emerges when aesthetics (hopefully) also deals with the everyday, having incorporated its motifs within itself yet without making them become essential characteristics of the aesthetic. And it is exactly this anti-essentialist perspective that we would like to promote here. This paragraph, yet, should be understood as a sort of "interlude" within our wider treatment of the question of the aesthetics of Experience Design. It will be limited to a brief overview — hopefully not too hasty for the reader who is encountering the topic for the first time — while focusing the analysis on some critical remarks on Everyday Aesthetics' overall development concerning specifically its relationship with aestheticization phenomena. For a more detailed analysis of Everyday Aesthetics and its agenda and concepts we refer the reader to the various volumes and essays quoted in the course of this paragraph, and also to the reconstruction provided in Iannilli (2019a), where the metaphor of a person's maturation process through the stages of infancy, adolescence, and adulthood has been used. This interlude is part of the wider research I previously carried out there and based specifically on Everyday Aesthetics' literature. Hence, the impression it might give is that of referencing more the scholarship rather than "the world". Yet, we believe that tracking and clarifying the theoretical structures each time underlying Everyday Aesthetics can tell us something on the ways both aesthetics and the everyday are conceived of by those who have dealt with these topics recently, and hence can contribute to a better understanding of these conceptions' limits and potential.

With Everyday Aesthetics we are referring to that sub-discipline of philosophical aesthetics generally devoted to the analysis of the aesthetic characters and implications of everyday experience.

The interest in this topic and the programmatic commitment to establishing a corresponding and somehow "official" line of research can be identified in the 1990s of the 20th century. Yet, there is no shortage of examples prior to that period in the history of philosophy. Just think of the research done by Georg Simmel and Walter Benjamin, to mention only two of the most renowned authors in this respect. Our usage of the specific label in capital letters is hence aimed at distinguishing Everyday Aesthetics as a historical specification of a disciplinary interest in the everyday and its aesthetic quality. Several factors have contributed to the development of this line of research. Among the most relevant ones, according to Leddy (2012), are the renewed interest in Deweyan aesthetics, the narrowing of the boundary between "high arts" and "popular arts", the formulation of an aesthetics focused on environmental issues (environmental aesthetics) and of feminist aesthetics, and the dialogue between Western and non-Western philosophical traditions. To this canonical list of factors we could add two points of great importance: the impact of digital technologies that have apparently deconstructed and restructured every area of our experience, and the indisputable fact that it is precisely since the 1990s that all over the world, in every philosophical, analytical and continental tradition, there has been a revival of attention to the 18th century and more particularly Baumgartenian origin of aesthetics as a theory of sensory perception.[36] This retrieval has been indeed problematic *per se*, but perhaps it has also been a symptom of the need for a new beginning outside the consolidated philosophy of art that has predominated in the two centuries that have followed since then. The 1990s, however, are in general also the context in which various investigations relating to the rise, configuration, and prevalence of the aesthetic as a value orienting individual and social dynamics, that is, investigations relating to aestheticization, began to appear. Despite this common territory, the relationship between Everyday Aesthetics and aestheticization is decidedly controversial. We will

---

36   See Adler (2002), as a paradigmatic example written in the wake of the significant debate, then in course for at least a decade, on the aesthetic thought preceding Kant and the narrowing of aesthetics to the philosophy of art.

return to this point later; for the moment it is enough to say that the general question of aestheticization has been "the incubator", the milieu in which Everyday Aesthetics has *de facto* thrived.

There are many scholars who have dealt with everyday aesthetic experience to a greater or lesser extent. However, they can be classified into two main categories, that is, classified as "continuists" or as "discontinuists"[37] depending on their stance towards the traditional aesthetics of art. Generally speaking, to be a continuist or discontinuist everyday aesthetician corresponds to the greater or lesser willingness to articulate an Everyday Aesthetics as a philosophical sub-discipline with common or distinctive characteristics with respect to established aesthetics. It also corresponds to the greater or lesser conviction that everyday aesthetic experience is a specific area with exclusive characteristics as compared to those found in other areas of aesthetic experience. Some names recur in these debates: Yuriko Saito, Arto Haapala, Thomas Leddy, Ossi Naukkarinen and Kevin Melchionne.[38] Saito (2007; 2017) develops an aesthetics in which the intertwining between ethical and aesthetic aspects of everyday life experience are crucial for the project of a better world-making. Haapala (2005), following a Heideggerian-existentialist ontology, advocates an Everyday Aesthetics which relies on the absence of extraordinariness linked to the process of familiarization, and therefore to the acquisition of a sense of belonging and identity in relation to a place. Leddy (2012) has two specific focuses: on aesthetic properties (he advocates an expansion of their range) and on a phenomenological understanding of the notion of aura (Leddy 2012: 127–49). Naukkarinen (2013) carries out a clear analysis of the ways in which the everyday unfolds and what its aesthetic specificity is, which he then applies to crucial issues discussed within Everyday Aesthetics. As we have already seen, the everyday, according to him, has a strongly relational nature:

---

37 Other labels used to discern among the various attempts to deal with the aesthetics of the everyday have been, for instance "expansionist" or "restrictivist", "weak pole" or "stance" or "strong pole" or "stance".

38 While Leddy (1995), Light and Smith (2005), Mandoki (2007) and, again, Saito (2007) are the seminal texts that have spurred Everyday Aesthetics' first development phases, this development has been "tracked" in such entries as Irvin (2009), Sartwell (2010), Livingston (2012) and Saito (2015).

although it has rather stable characteristics it can change over time running on a spectrum that equally includes positive, negative, and neutral features of experience. Melchionne (2014) maintains that the everyday aesthetic has an intrinsic relevance and value as compared to artistic value, since it has a great impact on the quality of subjective life, that is, on that which he defines as "subjective well-being".

If we consider these theoretically quite marked positions in addition to a number of diverse contributions on topics ranging from urban spaces to domestic practices, cultural places, and forms of entertainment, the impression we get is that of a sort of enthusiastic "hunt for the aesthetic",[39] wherever it may hide. In this framework, yet, problems started to surface when, in the wake of this enthusiastic recognition of the importance of the aesthetic in and for our experience, the task became capturing the aesthetic specificity of these "aesthetic reserves". In fact, the various positions recalled (again, if we take into consideration also the wider production of essays dealing with Everyday Aesthetics) did not generally create a common horizon that could even become the perimeter of a discipline endowed with a coherent theoretical profile. Moreover, each one for themselves has usually set individual concepts often without critically deepening their own historical-philosophical references (a different tendency can be identified in Leddy, for instance, who is perhaps the most extensively theoretically engaged everyday aesthetician). But this is a choice linked to the more or less theoretical tension or to the more or less practical aim connoting the proposed research. Both of these "sides" of research are important in themselves and as such are to be taken into due consideration. However, a potential risk is implied by this lack of cohesion. The risk is that to the extent that one works only on the everyday as *partis pris* it becomes difficult to see its many ramifications towards other experiential dimensions

---

39   Although it deviates from the specific field of investigation here under study, there is an Italian attempt, exemplifying this trend, to deal with the aesthetics of the everyday in this way. The reference is to Muccioli (2011), which examines nineteen "masterpieces of the aesthetics of everyday life", from the ball of yarn to the curl of butter, passing through the grain of dust, the tines of the fork, the twisted candle, etc. For a presentation of the various topics of Everyday Aesthetics see, in Italian, Di Stefano (2017).

(social, mental, cognitive, cultural ones, etc.), which relationally constitute the everyday. This fall out happens when the latter is hypostatized.

There is almost the impression that the everyday aesthetic appears in some of these descriptions — especially in those provided by the "discontinuist" stances — as a newly discovered world. Thus, an intentionally naive attitude can be identified in Everyday Aesthetics at least in its very beginning, a pseudo naivety that, as phenomenology teaches, is intrinsically dogmatic and therefore indeed hypostatizes the phenomenon. The latter consequently loses precisely the relational component and intersubjective texture that instead characterize it, if for no other reason than the fact that it is a primarily experiential dimension. Often, in the perspectives of Everyday Aesthetics, the experience that is taken into consideration is in fact entrenched within individual subjectivity, almost to the point of configuring a sort of methodological individualism. From this point of view Kevin Melchionne's approach is certainly exemplary, as it, with its tendency to identify Everyday Aesthetics with subjective well-being, is inclined to a psychological approach.

Due to this strategy of isolation of the phenomenon, one could go so far as to argue that Everyday Aesthetics risks having the very drawback of being exclusively, and somewhat restrictively, an Everyday Aesthetics, instead of being a general aesthetics that also deals with everyday life. And this is not a secondary issue, as it also has a heavy impact on the conceptualizations involved. Therefore, sometimes isolated from the relevant general historical-theoretical contexts, these concepts can appear to be derived directly from the phenomena and not properly as theoretical structures aware of their own grammar and put in relation with the phenomena sought to analyze.

While this has been true in large part for some of the authors who marked the first phase of Everyday Aesthetics' development, it is also true that a need to go deeper into the specificity of the aesthetic in relation to the everyday has been recognized. Recently, in fact, other authors have taken part in the discussion on Everyday Aesthetics by promoting a so-called "normative turn" — a shift that took place between 2010 and 2016 through studies carried out by Dowling (2010), Ratiu (2013), Forsey (2014) and Matteucci (2016).

These authors committed themselves to finding a criterion both selective and constitutive of aesthetic experience understood as intersubjective experience at a verbal, explicit and/or a non-verbal, implicit level. It is not our aim to take a stance on each of their proposals, but what we deem important is that they emphasized the general feature of intersubjectivity. The latter is here meant as a relational feature of aesthetic experience entailing an exchange between actors and between actors and (social) environments, where a tension between universality and particularity is at stake. These authors committed themselves to taking up the challenge of the descriptions and also of the cues provided by the major authors of the previous phase of Everyday Aesthetics,[40] however, while trying to bring the problem of Everyday Aesthetics within a more general reconsideration with a broader horizon. They dealt with the same analyses and the same phenomenology of the everyday, but in a different way, by deepening the question of the specificity of the everyday aesthetic. They did not examine the everyday *per se*, but the everyday as a qualifying moment of a wider and more complex discourse. At times, however, this has been done in an irreducibly "art-centered" perspective, that is, in a way that clearly sets the discourse in the extreme direction of a substantiation of Everyday Aesthetics through consolidated criteria of aesthetic experience and art criticism, as has been the case with Christopher Dowling.

By rightly wanting to break away from a philosophical aesthetics reductively constrained within the philosophy of art, Everyday Aesthetics has therefore in general — and perhaps necessarily, as it is almost always the case with breaking points within traditions — exceeded in its attempt to enucleate an alternative domain to consolidated aesthetics. This, in its first phase, made Everyday Aesthetics little attentive to the contextuality of the phenomenon

---

40   Please note that the distinctions here made between a "first phase" and a "second phase" of Everyday Aesthetics is meant to mark in a hopefully clear manner the "steps" of its development. Sometimes boundaries and labels can be murky, and in this case this means that authors belonging to the second phase have also contributed in the first one and that some of the authors of the first phase, such as Leddy and Naukkarinen, for instance, have since the beginning tried to clarify issues that were then also taken up in Everyday Aesthetics' further development.

it investigated — the aesthetic — even if by emphasizing the latter's pertinence to the everyday. This is reflected in Everyday Aesthetics' unresolved relationship with its own milieu, aestheticization.

Due attention should be paid to the fact that Everyday Aesthetics has been actually a way of responding to a need to reconsider aesthetics starting from aestheticization. Indeed, one could argue that, by paying high prices at least sometimes in terms of alienation, aestheticization as such already emancipates aesthetics from a segregation within the boundaries of art. Consequently, Everyday Aesthetics has been more a symptom than an antidote to aestheticization, as it has often believed to be, if it is true that most of the authors who have dealt with Everyday Aesthetics so far had mainly a contrasting, almost "therapeutic" attitude towards it.

Everyday Aesthetics' usual attitude towards aestheticization is further justified exactly in this respect. In fact, some of the theorists of Everyday Aesthetics on the one hand recognize and even emphasize the diffusion of the aesthetic beyond any culturally predetermined boundaries, but, on the other hand, they almost seem to demonize the very fact that aestheticization is a process or even a series of processes (see Welsch 1996) with an intrinsically artificial character. It seems almost as if this mistrust concerning the artificiality of aestheticization reflects the same pseudo naivety mentioned above. A pseudo naivety leading one to presuppose the diffusion of the aesthetic as a sort of natural datum. In that case the everyday aesthetic would dissolve from experience when manipulated even in the slightest way. The everyday as aesthetic hence seems to be assumed as a given, positum, even dogma of experience, confirming our suspicion of a tendentially non-relational conception of experiential structures.

However, it must be recognized that, perhaps in dialogue with those who proposed the normative turn, some early everyday aestheticians have recently changed their views on the question of aestheticization. Everyday Aesthetics seems to have mitigated its "frenzy" towards a (aesthetic) brave, or rather, brand new world.

To better clarify this passage, one could resort to the extreme cases of the evolution (or persistence) of the stances adopted over the years by Yuriko Saito and Thomas Leddy, excellent representatives respectively of a discontinuist and a continuist approach to Everyday Aesthetics. They also represent, respectively, those two types of choices mentioned above that are each committed to the more practical and to the more theoretical side of the issue. The testbeds are two contributions made by each of the two scholars in a "pre" and "post" normative turn phase. In the case of the work of the former (Saito 2007; 2017) the priority of the primarily ethical-ecological component that emerges strongly in the pages of her first volume is strengthened in the second one, which even dedicates a section to the "consequences of aesthetics" in the everyday (Saito 2017: 145–91). It is not surprising that a certain emphasis is placed on the moral consequences of what Saito herself defines as "consumerist aesthetics"[41]: a true list of "contraindications" of a non-ethically oriented use of the aesthetic. On the other hand, Thomas Leddy presents a more articulated position. He began (Leddy 2012) with an oppositional attitude towards aestheticization,[42] but then (Leddy 2018) criticized Saito's most recent perspective for not taking into due consideration the themes involved in aestheticization,[43] thus

---

41   In this regard we would also like to refer the reader to a 2018 text by Saito devoted extensively to the issue of aesthetic consumption and which we will take briefly into account here in the last chapter.

42   "Commercialization is probably thought bad because it encourages consumers to revel in shallow pleasures at the expense of ones that are deeper and more fulfilling. I wouldn't want to lend intellectual support to that!" (Leddy 2012: 210).

43   "In chapter 6 'Consequences of Everyday Aesthetics' Saito stresses the ways in which 'seemingly trivial and inconsequential aesthetic preference and taste have unexpected serious implications that determine the state of the world and the quality of life'. She calls this 'the power of the aesthetic'. The aesthetic can guide our behavior, our decisions and our actions. Although I disagree with little in this chapter, the mood of the first part can be kind of depressing. One begins to feel that aesthetics is, overall, a bad thing, since it is associated so strongly with propaganda, advertising and various forms of manipulation. [...] Another thing that is nagging me takes off from a sentence on consumerism that goes: 'Contemporary persuaders consist of qualities such as new, fashionable, cool, cutting-edge, novel, state-of-the-art, and stylish'. (146) The quote actually comes right after a quote from my book. So I may be expressing here some doubts about my own previously expressed views. I agree with Saito that obsession with these things can lead to bad consequences. But I also don't want to abandon these everyday aesthetic concepts, or demote them to the realm of the negative. So here is my thought, or perhaps it is just a worry. It seems to me that most of us participate in consumerism, although often with reservations. I might buy something partly because it is stylish for example. To that extent I

doing full justice to his declaredly continuist orientation. As we will see in the last chapter of the essay, a similar but more programmatic criticism has also been made by Naukkarinen. Furthermore, for an analysis addressing in a constructive way the relationship between aestheticization and reflectivity, we refer the reader to Matteucci (2017).

Actually, not only Leddy, but also other authors have at least in very recent years grasped the instances that have promoted this theoretical and problematic expansion and therefore have developed a more constructive perspective also towards the phenomena of aestheticization. They did so perhaps independently of the normative turn but, in any case, in a time consistent with its formulation. It is noteworthy, moreover, that this normative turn implies a somewhat sui generis normativity because in general it points towards greater dynamism in the understanding of Everyday Aesthetics in a continuist and intersubjective, therefore anti-essentialist sense. Haapala (2017), for example, no longer recognizes himself in a clearly discontinuist stance, but is open to considering the continuity and therefore the lack of a hierarchy between various spheres and levels of aesthetic experience. Although his standpoint is always very sensitive to the specificity of the context each time investigated, not least in its aestheticized connotation, already since Naukkarinen (1998), also Naukkarinen (2014; 2016;[44] 2017; 2018;[45] 2019), has focused more and more

---

might be buying into (literally) what the advertisers who use the 'aesthetic persuaders' want. But also I want this stylish item (say a nice pair of shoes), and I actually do think that they will look good on me. Even though I happily join in with critics of consumerist society, I cannot fully do so since I am part of it, and not just part of it out of 'no other choice'. I am part of it out of choices I make every day. I choose, for example, to shop at Whole Earth rather than Safeway. I choose to buy Ritual coffee over Seattle's Best, and I am not going to be seriously put off if I hear this described as fashionable. I am particularly susceptible to the persuader 'cool.' Most people I know want to be cool, or at least not to be 'uncool'. Even if I were to join a commune in the woods I would still need to buy certain products, and my choice of this lifestyle might well itself be the result of coming to see this lifestyle as stylish, although in a non-standard way" (see Leddy, May 2018: aestheticstoday.blogspot.com/2018/05/saito-and-thick-vs-thin-appreciation.html [accessed 4 April 2020]).

44 This essay has been co-authored with Johanna Bragge.

45 This essay has been co-authored with Darius Pacauskas.

openly on the aesthetic content of above all social behaviors, but also on the disciplinary status of aesthetics in relation to the rise of the so-called digital humanities and, more generally, to the implications of the relationship between individuals and digital devices, or machines, but this is not surprising. Melchionne (2017), finally, combines together the question of subjective well-being, aesthetic choice and the construction of taste through the algorithmic component of the digitalized experience. In this regard, it is interesting to note that today these themes linked to an experiential restructuring, starting from digitalization, but also from consumption dynamics, are dealt with in research fields linked, for example, to atmospherological aesthetics and the new theories of the mind. These may perhaps then become strategic references for Everyday Aesthetics, as they are active in its own milieu, and with whom it would be interesting to establish a dialogue that would probably be useful for all parties involved. What emerges is, in fact, a sort of "compensatory", so to speak, relationship between these three lines of research. On the one hand, atmospherological aesthetics and Everyday Aesthetics share the same starting point: everyday aesthetic experience; however, atmospherological aesthetics emphasizes the pathic component of aesthetic experience, which entails an almost total "passivization" of the experiencing subject, but at the same time widely deals with, by not necessarily demonizing it, the theme of aestheticization. (Interestingly, it raises the problem of the producibility or designability of atmospheres for example in Böhme 2001 — who talks about a true "aesthetic work"). In this sense, Everyday Aesthetics in its more "activist" side could learn to mitigate its generally pathological vision of aestheticization, recognizing how everyday experience also implies a certain passivity, a "letting oneself be taken in" by the situations one finds oneself in. Conversely, atmospherology could learn from a relationally amended Everyday Aesthetics to mitigate some excesses due to its own pathic perspective (see Griffero 2019). On the other hand, the new theories of the mind are based on a strongly relational component in the development of the extended mind problem, yet at the same time leaving aside almost entirely the analysis of the specifically aesthetic component of experience, due to an understandable emphasis on the cognitive. In this sense

Everyday Aesthetics would find confirmation of the usefulness of a relational conception of experience and, symmetrically, the new theories of the mind would find useful clues for the development of theses that take into account the role of the aesthetic in the constitution of the mind as extended, embedded, enactive and embodied.

More generally, it is interesting to mention some attempts, all of which appeared in 2017, therefore in a fully "post" normative turn phase, to distinguish and link different but related levels in which everyday experience would take place. First of all we can mention Haapala (2017), in partial continuity with Haapala (2005), where a distinction is proposed between a "lived world", or individual level of experience, and a "life world", or collective, cultural, social level of experience. The two levels are intertwined into a circular relationship based on the temporal aspect of experience; then we can recall the already introduced Naukkarinen and Vasquez (2017)[46] in which a distinction is made between a "daily life" experience and an "everyday" experience. The former is understood as a non-thematized background imbued with routines, the latter as the emergence from the almost imperceptible flow of routine of a particular type of pattern that corresponds to the everyday. We can then recall Ratiu (2017) resorting to a Gadamerian (see Gadamer 1960) phenomenological-hermeneutical reading of the notions of *Erlebnis* as a lived and immediate experience in which consciousness is intentionally directed to phenomena, and of *Erfahrung* as an experience derived from an interpretive activity that occurs temporally. Both of them would be equally part of the *Lebenswelt* of which also Ratiu then emphasizes both the individual and cultural-intersubjective dimension. One can therefore speak in this regard of a further development of Everyday Aesthetics, if not even of its germinal evolution into a general aesthetics.

Conversely, a countertendency to this process can be found in a particular editorial endeavor. At the beginning of 2018, the prestigious journal *The Monist* (see MacBride and Haldane 2018) devoted a special issue to the topics in question, titling it *The Aesthetics of Everyday Life*. On the one hand it recognized the

---

46   Making some of the contents developed in Naukkarinen (2013) more
      explicit.

urgent need to deal with these topics, but on the other hand it almost neglected thirty years of research carried out in the field of Everyday Aesthetics. From the overall analysis of this issue there emerges an attempt to mark a new beginning in the debate born around the aesthetic–everyday nexus, signaling a sort of new pseudo naivety, a sort of pseudo naivety "squared", about the everyday. It is striking, moreover, that the title echoes that of a now historical anthology edited fifteen years ago by Andrew Light and Jonathan Smith (see Light and Smith 2005), when Everyday Aesthetics itself was in the midst of its maturation process, still moving with uncertainty between various possible labels. Indeed, considering also some internal limits of Everyday Aesthetics, some kind of overcoming or rethinking of it might be necessary. In the case in question, however, this happens, *de facto*, by disqualifying it altogether, through an act of removal that seems almost ideological, not in terms of a perspective opening. The contributions included in this issue of *The Monist* can be identified into four main general areas of interest: the relationship between aesthetics and the ethical-social aspects of everyday experience; the analysis of some emblematical phenomena for an aesthetics of everyday life; the relationship between art and quotidianity; the conditions of possibility of aesthetic experiences. And these are generally also the topics Everyday Aesthetics has dealt with. Yet, the result is a sort of descriptivism that is for the most part morally oriented and in many ways similar to that already characterizing various studies related to Everyday Aesthetics and which it would be a task to correct with a critical rather than with an ideological attitude. The decision to avoid any comparison with a line of research that, for better or worse, has been consolidated in recent decades therefore makes various analyses documented in *The Monist* appear to a certain extent naive, although capable of interesting ideas but rarely able to put forward theoretical developments that can enrich the aesthetic considerations on the (common) issues in question. A somewhat high price paid to the desire for a new beginning, for this field of aesthetics, in the nominal change that from the thematization of "the everyday" shall lead to the analysis of "everyday life".

Contrary to what *The Monist* has done, it seems right, instead, to acquire the heritage that comes from Everyday Aesthetics' descriptions and reflections. This heritage, however, should be rethought in a broader sense both as far as its references and its theoretical and methodological frameworks are concerned. To the same extent, the everyday should be recovered and used in its fundamental role as a relational element necessary for the understanding of the structures of experience, but not considered as an autonomous resolutive principle.

Everyday Aesthetics, therefore, is (or has been) a symptom of the crisis of the Western theory of experience, not its resolution point: a gentle travel companion from which one shall bid farewell.

2.

JOHN DEWEY: FORM AS FUNCTION

2.1. *An Experiment*

Art as Experience is John Dewey's 1934 book on aesthetics. On the one hand this work presents the central issues that can be generally found in Dewey's research: social criticism, education, philosophical reform and knowledge. On the other hand it can be read as the apex and the *hapax* of a very specific path shaped by a growing interest in the nexus between expression — as something which is not merely subjective nor denotative — and perception — as something which is not merely passive nor instantaneous. This nexus can be understood as a very important feature of Dewey's essentially anti-dualistic and processual conception of experience as an immersive (i.e. overarching and thickly mediated) interaction (i.e. a biunivocal, mutual relationship) between an organism and an environment. This immersive interaction, though, is not simple as it implies a rhythm[1] made of disharmony and harmony,

---

1   Rhythm is a key notion for Dewey. It lies at the heart of his conception of experience and Dewey constantly makes reference to it in *Art as Experience*. In particular in its seventh and eighth chapters (respectively, "The Natural History of Form", Dewey 1934: 139–66, and "The Organization of Energies", Dewey 1934: 167–90), the two immediately following "Substance and Form", the chapter we are going to delve into in this section of the book, rhythm is unequivocally thematized as "an essential property of form" (Dewey 1934: 152), as a true and proper material, relational, temporal, historical and synaesthetic principle of experience. "The first characteristic of the environing world that makes possible the existence of artistic form is rhythm. There is rhythm in nature before poetry, painting, architecture and music exist. Were it not so, rhythm as an essential property of form would be merely superimposed upon material,

need and desire, fractures and saturations. From this point of view, it somehow recalls the dialectics between problem setting and problem solving mentioned earlier.

In *Art as Experience* all this is addressed in a particular way. Experience, when aesthetic, is properly "an" experience. It is discerned from our generic experience by having the feature of being a gratifying experience in which some features of the latter are qualitatively intensified, or made more perspicuous and conspicuous. In these terms, "an" experience is defined by

---

not an operation through which material effects its own culmination in experience. [...] As I pointed out, [rhythms] are the conditions of form in experience and hence of expression. But an esthetic experience, the work of art in its actuality, is perception. Only as these rhythms, even if embodied in an outer object that is itself a product of art, become a rhythm in experience itself are they esthetic. And this rhythm in what is experienced is something quite different from intellectual recognition that there is rhythm in the external thing. [...] Rhythm involves constant variation. In the definition that was given of rhythm as ordered variation of manifestation of energy, variation is not only. as important as order, but it is an indispensable coefficient of esthetic order. The greater the variation, the more interesting the effect, provided order is maintained — a fact that proves that the order in question is not to be stated in terms of objective regularities but requires another principle for its interpretation. This principle, once more, is that of cumulative progression toward the fulfillment of an experience in terms of the integrity of the experience itself — something not to be measured in external terms, though not attainable without the use of external materials, observed or imagined. [...] There is, of course, no rhythm without recurrence. [...] Esthetic recurrence is that of *relationships* that sum up and carry forward. Esthetic recurrence in short is vital, physiological, functional. Relationships rather than elements recur, and they recur in differing contexts and with different consequences so that each recurrence is novel as well as a reminder. In satisfying an aroused expectancy, it also institutes a new longing, incites a fresh curiosity, establishes a changed suspense. The completeness of the integration of these two offices, opposed as they are in abstract conception, by the same means instead of by using one device to arouse energy and another to bring it to rest, measures artistry of production and perception. What has been said may seem to exaggerate the temporal aspect of perception. I have, without doubt, stretched out elements that are usually more or less telescoped. But in no case can there be perception of an object except in a process developing in time. Mere excitations, yes; but not an object as perceived, instead of just recognized as one of a familiar kind. If our view of the world consisted of a succession of momentary glimpses, it would be no view of the world nor of anything in it" (Dewey 1934: 152, 165, 169, 174, 179).

Dewey also as conscious. It is important to note, though, that the term "conscious" here should not be read as describing a fixed or absolute feature of aesthetic experience. It does not refer to a Cartesian transparency, neither is it an element that marks a specific ontological region. Quite the contrary: in a Deweyan fashion consciousness can be understood as a sort of indicator that our experience is taking a specific form that fits us, that works for us. It is as a stance, not necessarily a verbal one, that we take towards our generic experience. Consciousness is always rapidly changing, as it connotes the level where the formed disposition and the immediate situation touch and interact. It is the ongoing adjustment of the self *and* the world in experience. It is interaction between historicity, contingency and progress, orientation and expectation. As Dewey says:

> 'Consciousness' is the more acute and intense in the degree of the readjustments that are demanded, approaching the nil as the contact is frictionless and interaction fluid. It is turbid when meanings are undergoing reconstruction in an undetermined direction, and becomes clear as a decisive meaning emerges. (Dewey 1934: 270)

However, according to Dewey, "an experience" is not a radically different kind of experience. Rather, it emerges as a particular articulation of the generic flow of our experience, while at the same time being continuous with it. It is a "focused" experience which yet is "happily flowing".[2]

A way to visualize, so to speak, Dewey's conception of experience, in general, and aesthetic experience, in particular, could be that of a spectrum with internal gradations which can be(come) more or less intense, saturated, dense or, as we will see, "consummated". In this framework, art plays an exemplary role precisely in this sense: it provides a "con-densed" form of "an" experience by intensifying certain elements that would otherwise remain implicit, or at least potential in experience. This recalls the dialectics between thematization, intensification and operativity mentioned earlier. Yet, according to Dewey, works of art should

---

2 Csikszentmihalyi (i.e. 1990; 1996; 1998) has addressed this topic from a positive psychology point of view.

not be considered as isolated objects but as new ways of "seeing" (or of perceiving the expressiveness of) things that we encounter in our experience, which need an interaction (or a pole that perceives their expressiveness) in order to be "activated".

Especially from a specifically aesthetic standpoint, isolation is not an option for Dewey. Not only works of art are part of our common world, but so is the material that they are made of, and their (sense) qualities *and* meanings that are perceived immediately by the cooperating senses of an organism situated or embedded within and interacting with, an environment. From an aesthetic standpoint they can be considered as experiential devices that stem out from experience and have the capacity to generate new experiences. Dewey's emphasis is neither on subjects nor on objects or on isolated (i.e. ab-solute, hypostatized) elements as such, but rather on experience as a whole.

The key feature that distinguishes the Deweyan approach can be defined, not coincidentally, continuism. Despite the positive aspects of Dewey's anti-essentialist approach, aimed at reestablishing the nexus between "ordinary" experience and "intensified" experience, there has been plenty of criticism against him. In particular these criticisms have been put forward by various scholars who, in recent years, have advocated a reconsideration and a downsizing of the centrality of art in aesthetics. In the face of a project of institution of an Everyday Aesthetics, at the end of the day for some of these theoreticians[3] Dewey would do nothing but perpetrating the traditional equation of aesthetics with a philosophy of art. Yet, as we have seen above at the end of the first chapter, in a number of contributions Dewey is still described as one of the unquestionable founding fathers of this new sub-discipline of aesthetics.[4] It should be understood, however, how for Dewey art has an *exemplary* and not an *exclusive* role and how, for him, there is no total overlap, or reducibility, but a continuity, between the artistic and the

---

3   See at least Saito (2007), but in general all those contributions authored by so-called "strong pole", or "discontinuist" everyday aestheticians who attempt to emphasize, at least in a first phase of development of Everyday Aesthetics as we have seen in paragraph 1.6., an account of the everyday and its aesthetics considered in its "pure" everydayness.

4   See at least Irvin (2009); Sartwell (2010); Leddy (2012).

aesthetic. Such continuity, moreover, is as strong as to some extent desirable and not simply given. This point is revealed by the related issue, that Dewey is well aware of, regarding the possibility of learning how to experience, of a betterment of experience. The first term, "artistic", would have more to do with what is intentionally and productively accomplished, while the second one, "aesthetic", refers

> to experience as appreciative, perceiving, and enjoying. It denotes the consumer's rather than the producer's standpoint. [Yet], the relation that exists in having an experience between doing and undergoing, indicate that the distinction between esthetic and artistic cannot be pressed so far as to become a separation. (Dewey 1934: 53)

A testbed to prove the adequacy of this thesis could consist in replacing Dewey's use of the term "artist" or "producer" with "aesthetically competent individual", and his use of the concept of "work of art" with "aesthetic device". In the first case, the advantage would be to focus not so much on the figure of the artist as such but, actually, on a certain type of competence that in the aesthetic dimension can intervene in the management of the material of one's own experience. The focus is not on the "who" as such, but on the "how" a certain individual operates. In the second case, the environmental, interactive and verbal understanding of experience that characterizes Dewey's conception, but also our approach to Experience Design, would be maintained. The well-known verbal acceptation with which Dewey describes the mind can certainly be mentioned here, and last but not least the verbal acceptation with which he understands a "work" of art and with which we have also understood the "works" of design in this essay. The focus is therefore not on the "what" as such, but again, on the "how".

However, the aim of this chapter is certainly not to formulate a defense of Dewey's position towards its most recent misinterpretations.[5] What is important here is rather to show how

---

5   For an accurate analysis defending *Art as Experience* see at least Puolakka (2014; 2015) and Matteucci (2016).

a particular understanding of at least part of *Art as Experience* in the sense we recommend can also provide interesting indications for the theme at the center of this essay, namely the aesthetics of Experience Design. We will attempt at doing so while also answering some of the questions that emerged towards the end of the previous chapter.

The entire Deweyan project in philosophy is aimed at restoring the experiential continuity of what, due to a basically dualistic Western metaphysical tradition, has been customarily treated as separate. Subject and object, mind and body, sense and meaning, perception and expression, substance and form are just some of the elements that Dewey analyzes in their con-fusion. One could say that Dewey's challenge is to overcome dichotomies that, as far as experience *qua* experience is concerned, do not subsist. Dewey's theory of (aesthetic) experience is based on the ongoing cross-layering of levels, which can be analytically distinguished, but experientially (i.e. in the actual experience) are con-fused with each other. Again, the idea of a spectrum with internal gradations comes in handy to explain Dewey's distinctive approach. Rather than dichotomies, then, in Dewey we may speak of antinomic polarities, which he addresses while being aware that every subsequent analysis of experience *qua* experience inevitably and forcedly reduces the vigor, complexity and the cooperation of energies that connote experience as such.

In particular, we may subsume these polarities under two main poles, one tending towards explicitness, thematization, and the other one tending towards implicitness, operativity. Yet, it is precisely that idea of "intensification" mentioned earlier that makes their relationship non-dualistic, as far as an aesthetic/qualitative viewpoint is concerned.

2.2. *Three False Hiatuses*

It would be impossible to reconstruct here in detail the analysis of the various traditional and encrusted dualisms that Dewey fights against. Yet, a way to approach coherently with our aims his challenge to overcome such dualisms could be stressing three main hiatuses that Dewey deals with.

The first one concerns the relationship between producer and consumer and between ordinary and aesthetic experience:

> [...] the conditions that create the gulf which exists generally between producer and consumer in modern society operate to create also a chasm between ordinary and esthetic experience. (Dewey 1934: 15)

According to a canonical view, the competence in the management of experiential material would seem to be delegated and limited to "those who produce" and not recognized to "those who consume". In this sense, a "user", an ordinary "consumer", would not have aesthetic experiences in the proper sense, because her/his experiences would lack the nexus of activity and passivity that characterizes "an" experience as aesthetic. For Dewey, instead, the distinction between producer and user is not related to characters owned by the former and denied to the other, but is a matter of degree. In this spectrum of continuity or, say, graduality it is true that — once again — the artist as well as the work of art play an exemplary role, but not in the sense, however, of establishing an isolated region populated by individuals and objects that exclusively have a certain quality. Being an "artist" in the management of something should be understood instead as an adjectival qualification, in the same way as being a "master" of something, or "mastering" something, can be. The idea of competence that can be drafted from these considerations is that the (aesthetically) competent individual as a producer can manage or handle what happens already in the anonymous, confused, oblique, and highly facilitated designed forms of everydayness, where a flow of sense emerges without us, as consumers, generally being able to get a handle of it. The (aesthetically) competent individual, contrariwise, is able to perform gestures that can be both deliberate and automatic, depending on the degree of incorporation of that particular competence. These gestures, yet, can still be defined as "artificial", because they are the outcome of processes, i.e. they are more or less "learned". The question is therefore not resolved in the mere contraposition between two kinds of competences, one that is perhaps more natural and the other more artificial. The sense of artificiality/naturality that the

carrying out of some competence elicits is due to the familiarity
with the processes that it embodies. In general, indeed, a trait
of the aesthetic is its ability to make appear what is artificially
constructed as natural, which implies an infinite scale of possible
degrees. The peculiarity of the aesthetically competent individual
is that s/he performs her/his competence as if it were "nature".
These questions are well presented in the next quotation from
Dewey, and they exemplify quite effectively how pressing it is for
him to resolve this and the following hiatuses.

> *If* artistic and esthetic quality is implicit in every normal
> experience, how shall we explain how and why it so generally fails
> to become explicit? Why is it that to multitudes art seems to be an
> importation into experience from a foreign country and the esthetic
> to be a synonym for something artificial? (Dewey 1934: 18)

The second hiatus concerns the relationship between what is
done explicitly/directly and what is done implicitly/indirectly in
the "artificial":

> In the [artificial] there is a split between what is overtly done and
> what is intended. [...] Wherever this split between what is done and
> its purpose exists, there is insincerity, a trick, a simulation of an
> act that intrinsically has another effect. When the natural and the
> cultivated blend in one, acts of social intercourse are works of art.
> (Dewey 1934: 69)

Here Dewey makes an honorific use of the term "artificial". It
has a negative connotation insofar as it indicates "insincerity".
We have made a descriptive use of it, in order to distinguish the
eminently "constructed" character of design in general and of
Experience Design in particular. This character is indeed implied
by a mediation of some kind that is performed by design, and
in particular Experience Design, on the materials of experience,
which should be something spontaneous — "natural" — so to
speak. At the same time, we have used the same term, just above,
to confer a processual character upon a certain kind of competence
that may emerge in some individuals in their management of
the experiential material with which they interact. Of course, a
distinction of this kind must be simply understood as a functional

one, i.e., as functional to the development of the discourse, and to the characterization of the particularities of its different levels.

The interweaving of these levels was in fact already extensively undertaken in the first chapter of the present essay in terms of a "cool design", i.e. a design in which the more the design of functions remains internal to the experiential field ("wherever [there is no] split between what is done and its purpose"), the more it is successful: namely, the more it makes appear as "natural" what we have called "artificial" and what Dewey describes here as "cultivated". The term "natural" should not be understood here as synonym with "given" or "essential", but as an adjective that says something about the relationship that exists, or the "transactions" — as Dewey would say — between human beings and the world, and in particular between an individual and a social context ("acts of social intercourse"). It also implies the situatedness and embeddedness of experience.[6]

> [N]aturalism in art [...] means that all which can be expressed is some aspect of the relation of man and his environment, and that this subject-matter attains its most perfect wedding with form when the basic rhythms that characterize the interaction of the two are depended upon and trusted with abandon. (Dewey 1934: 156)

"Cultivated" should be thus understood in this context as something that concerns the plane of implementation of the natural and that is continuous with it. We will get back to the nature of this implementation later in the chapter, when we will address more extensively the concept of aesthetic competence. Suffice it to quote for now a passage in which Dewey evidently criticizes a non-attentive, non-embedded, and non-particular approach in the management of "nature":

> the true antithesis of nature is not art but arbitrary conceit, fantasy, and stereotyped convention. (Dewey 1934: 156)

---

6   For a detailed contextualization of Dewey's naturalistic theory of intelligence in an empiricist metaphysics see Shook (2000: 240–69).

The third hiatus concerns the relationship between the aesthetic and the artistic:

> Were it true that only qualities coming to us through sense-organs in *isolation* are directly experienced, then, of course, all relational material would be super added by an association that is extraneous — or according to some theorists, by a 'synthetic' action of thought. [...] On this basis there is always a gap between the esthetic and the artistic. They are of two different kinds. (Dewey 1934: 123, 125)

This can be considered the "trickiest" of the three groups of hiatuses indicated. By saying that the aesthetic and the artistic "are of two different kinds", Dewey seems to be contradicting himself, as he previously stated that such distinction "cannot be pressed so far as to become a separation".[7] Actually, here Dewey is trying to show the inadequacy of two theories for the explanation of the dynamics of experience: the theory of sense data and associationism. In the first case, the relationship between expressiveness and perception is explicated on the basis of the fact that the single sense qualities that are directly perceived give expressiveness to things and events. In this case, qualities are hence "undergone". In the second case, the relationship between expressiveness and perception is explicated on the basis of the fact that the act of association (carried out by the subject) or the associated material, gives expressiveness to qualities. In this case, qualities are hence projected onto, and are far from being undergone.

The problem, for Dewey, is that none of these two theories takes into account the inextricable nexus between expression

---

7   An "awkwardness" that connotes to a certain extent this relationship is well summarized by the following quotation: "We have no word in the English language that unambiguously includes what is signified by the two words 'artistic' and 'esthetic'. Since 'artistic' refers primarily to the act of production and 'esthetic' to that of perception and enjoyment, the absence of a term designating the two processes taken together is unfortunate. Sometimes, the effect is to separate the two from each other, to regard art as something superimposed upon esthetic material, or, upon the other side, to an assumption that, since art is a process of creation, perception and enjoyment of it have nothing in common with the creative act. In any case, there is a certain verbal awkwardness in that we are compelled sometimes to use the term 'esthetic' to cover the entire field and sometimes to limit it to the receiving perceptual aspect of the whole operation" (Dewey 1934: 53).

and perception, and between doing and undergoing, that actually connotes experience. Therefore, what is neglected is the continuity relationship that exists between "the artistic" and the aesthetic, which do not coincide as such, but concern a multiplicity of different degrees of conspicuity. One degree tending towards the thematic/explicit, another tending towards the intensifying/inviting, and a third one tending towards the operative/implicit.[8]

2.3. *Substance and Form, Updated*

Dewey addresses exactly this latter hiatus in one of the central chapters of *Art as Experience* titled "Substance and Form" (Dewey 1934: 111–38). Interestingly, this chapter follows the two chapters devoted to the analysis of expression. At the same time, it also represents one extremely pregnant instance of the increasingly elaborated construction of a particular theory of aesthetic perception represented in general by *Art as Experience*. The problem of the nexus between expression and perception seems to find a quite privileged theoretical venue in these pages.

Art is the paradigm mainly analyzed by Dewey also in this chapter. Yet, the latter becomes particularly interesting also for the aesthetics of Experience Design insofar as, as we shall see, Dewey refers the problem of the end at which an aesthetic configuration aims in general to the relationship between substance and form. In other words, what becomes crucial here is the problem of the function that must be performed by an object or even experience,

---

8   "Both of the theories considered separate the live creature from the world in which it lives; lives by interaction through a series of related doings and undergoings, which when they are schematized by psychology, are motor and sensory. The first theory finds in organic activity isolated from the events and scenes of the world a sufficient cause of the expressive nature of certain sensations. The other theory locates the esthetic element 'solely in ourselves', through enacting of motor relations in 'shapes'. But the process of living is continuous; it possesses continuity because it is an everlastingly renewed process of acting upon the environment and being acted upon by it, together with institution of relations between what is done and what is undergone. Hence experience is necessarily cumulative and its subject matter gains expressiveness because of cumulative continuity" (Dewey 1934: 109).

but also by the environment with which we deal everyday. Objects, experiences, and environments that are constructed and realized through the design of functions.

The main theme of this chapter of *Art as Experience* is, in fact, the translatability of the expressiveness typical of a context — and, specifically, that belonging to the "common world" — into the expressiveness of another context — and specifically, that belonging to a very particular and individualized dimension in which something of the "common world" is absorbed and re-issued. Dewey develops this theme from the point of view of the relationship between substance and form and in such a way that it can be also read as a variation of the relationship between function — or "the what", the functional content, generally linked to instrumentality — and form — or "the how", the way things (are made) appear, generally linked to an aesthetic dimension. The following question summarizes well what Dewey aims at clarifying in this chapter:

> Is form, in its esthetic sense, something that uniquely marks off as esthetic from the beginning a certain realm of objects, or is it the abstract name for what emerges whenever an experience attains complete development? (Dewey 1934: 112)

For the question at issue here, Experience Design, this can be seen as the problem of the translatability of operative elements and structures that are implicit in common experience (where we "do" things without openly "labeling" them) into, using Dewey's terminology, "cultivated" or designed experiential configurations. These configurations, by providing pre-constituted experiential frameworks indeed quantify, that is to say thematize, "label", or make explicit to a certain extent, at least part of the contents of the aforementioned operative elements and structures.

Is the expressiveness of these operative elements and structures going to be arrested, and hence lost, when "crystallized", thematized in those configurations? How is it possible to generate new meanings when our everyday environments are widely designed?

In some cases and within certain limits, the [...] greater accommodation of man and environment to each other is unfavorable to further esthetic creation. Things are now too smooth; there is not enough irregularity to create demand for a new manifestation and opportunity for a new rhythm. [...] The environment is, in so far, exhausted, worn out, esthetically speaking. (Dewey 1934: 163)

Dewey, yet, seems to be optimistic about all this:

in time, this very familiarity sets up resistance in some minds. Familiar things are absorbed and become a deposit in which the seeds or sparks of new conditions set up a turmoil. (Dewey 1934: 163)

The answer, however, is to be found again in Dewey's "radical" (and not reductionist) continuism.

Dewey starts off his analysis of the relationship between substance and form by addressing the problem of the tension between self-expression or individuality, and material that belongs to the common world, in which this individuality is indeed situated and embedded.

The material belongs to the common world but the way to both express it and perceive it is individual, because the self assimilates this material in a peculiar way, sh/e personally processes it. The result of this activity of interaction with the material is relevant insofar as it does not have some fixed or pre-established characteristics in itself, but is capable of generating new experiences.

This dialectics could also be interpreted as the question of style. Style is something that can be ascribed to an individuality — which is therefore recognizable as such thanks to it — that nevertheless interacts with materials that belong to the common world and that the individual absorbs and eventually releases in specific ways — as is the case with the "style of an era", that is to say the style that characterizes the whole of the individual practices of a certain historical period which share a certain recognizable character.[9]

---

9   These passages are quite consonant with the contents developed in Simmel (1908), a cornerstone in the philosophical treatment of the problem of style, and in particular with the idea that style is something implying an irreducible dialectics between "individuality and universality".

In his analysis Dewey oscillates between the description of the producer's point of view and that of the percipient.

In the first case, the following claim may be indicative:

> The *material* [*scil.*: 'the what', the substance] out of which a work of art is composed belongs to the common world rather than to the self, and yet there is self expression in art because the self assimilates that material in a distinctive way to reissue it into the public world in a form that builds a new object. [...] The material expressed cannot be private; that is the state of the madhouse. But the manner of saying it is individual. (Dewey 1934: 112–3)

In the second case, we read:

> If he perceives esthetically, he will create an experience of which the intrinsic subject-matter, the substance, is new. [...] We live in the same old world, [yet] every individual brings with him, when he exercises his individuality, a way of seeing and feeling that in its interaction with old material creates something new, something not previously existing in experience. (Dewey 1934: 113)

Thus, the question of style concerns both a style of production and a style of perception. Moreover, these are endowed with a particular connotation, i.e. they can be acquired, learned, because they are the outcome of processes. These processes can be considered both on a spatial level — involving situatedness, or embeddedness — and on a temporal level — involving historicity.

In fact, what these passages make emerge is not only the tension between what's common and what's individual, but also between what's old and what's new, between a past and a dimension of novelty. This brings us closer to the clarification of the question of aesthetic competence that we have only sketched before.

What's "past" can in fact be conceived of in terms of "sedimented meaning" and what's "new" in terms of something that has to do with a "first hand", "personal", "contingent" experience (since it is informed by the contingent, that is to say situated and historical conditions of the interaction). In this sense what's new is not radically new but it has a certain feature of familiarity as far as it concerns the emergence *as meaningful* of something that has already been experienced. The relationship between these two planes pertains exactly to the intertwining due to the interaction between common, already existing and available material, and an individuality. In any case, it is useful to point out again that the creativity conveyed by design implies a different type of creativity than the one traditionally attributed to the creative individual as a genius and an *ex-nihilo* producer, that is to say a "demiurgical" or even a "Promethean" creativity. The type of creativity conveyed by design is instead of a "managerial" and "sustainable" type, since it deals with material which already exists and is included in particular situations. And, again, even though innovation is a fundamental part in design processes, it must be stressed that to "innovate", does not strictly mean to "invent", although an element of novelty is implied in both cases.

The point, for Dewey, is to adequately understand the conditions that make an aesthetic management of all this possible, that is, to understand how it is possible to acquire and carry out an ability to generate new meaning starting from relationships that have been crystallized in a form, in pre-constituted experiential frameworks.

Speaking of self-expression, of individuality, almost inevitably raises the question of intentionality. Yet, in the framework of Dewey's thought this concept can be accepted insofar as it is not meant as a fixed structure that can be reduced to an instantaneous (which does not mean contingent) dimension. Intentionality should be then understood as a dynamic structure that emerges processually, historically and, most importantly, as something that acts within horizons of potentiality of meaning, enhancing them on a case by case basis (see Dewey's example of the artist's intentions, Dewey 1934: 113–4). Anyway, rather than risking to stretch too much a concept that is particularly nuanced and charged with specific meanings, such as the concept of intentionality, we could here refer to something Dewey describes as "attentive perception".[10] By combining a dimension of responsiveness between activity (attentive) and passivity (perception), of situatedness or embeddedness, and of orientation — by past experiences, in actuality, towards the future, or what we expect it to be — in a similar way as what has been described as "consciousness" earlier,

---

10 Although along different lines, Nanay (2016) has developed a somewhat similar concept.

I claim that it is precisely through this concept that we can better understand Dewey's idea of aesthetic competence.

Dewey then provides a first definition of form:

> a substance so formed that it can enter into the experiences of others and enable them to have more intense and more *fully rounded out experiences* [emphasis added] of their own. (Dewey 1934: 114)

In this case it would seem legitimate to speak of a "formative capacity": form is substance that has the "ability" and the adequate "size" to provide enhanced, implemented experiences. The idea of a *fully rounded out experience* also seems to recall an important idea that already emerged in the previous chapter. What I am referring to is the idea of the configuration of "someone's everyday", of an "aesthetic niche", or of a "personal space" that, emerging from the potentialities of the "common world" as meaningful, we inhabit as our own.

> This is what it is to have form. It marks a way of envisaging, of feeling, and of presenting experienced matter so that it most readily and effectively becomes material for the construction of an adequate experience. (Dewey 1934: 114)

Having form concerns the ability to "see the face" ("envisage"), to perceive the expressiveness of the common world and to deal with it "adequately", that is, by following and caring for the trend lines that potentially innervate it and to use them in such a way that allows for a qualitatively enhanced experience to be constructed.

> Hence there can be no distinction drawn, save in reflection, between form and substance. The work itself is matter formed into esthetic substance. (Dewey 1934: 114)

In these lines the verbal acceptation that Dewey attributes to the word "work" strongly emerges, and it is also confirmed in the following lines by a similar analysis of what would be the "act" of the expression, where "act" should be referred here to the operative dimension of experience mentioned above. Both "work" and "act" are what they are by virtue of their *way of being*. This modal-verbal acceptation of the aesthetic construct is something that also characterizes Experience Design in the way it has been described earlier in this text. Experience Design "works" insofar as it does not concern single distinct objects; it works when it emphasizes an environmental dimension and/or concerning a device that is able to be conducive to an experience and to support it throughout its course.

> The act itself is *what* it is because of *how* it is done. In the act there is no distinction, but perfect integration of manner and content, form and substance. (Dewey 1934: 114)

A form, then, is not such if it hardens, stiffens in an object, but only if it becomes a potential that always prompts new experiences somehow similar to the experience that is enclosed in that particular construct. Form is thus no longer considered by Dewey in relation to the objectual content, but it is rather form of experience. Art has its own exemplarity in Dewey's discourse, but it must be noted that the relevance goes to the experiential construction and the main focus remains on interaction or experience which, as such, can also be an everyday experience.

> Form is a character of every experience that is an experience. Art in its specific sense enacts more deliberately and fully the conditions that effect this unity. *Form may then be defined as the operation of forces that carry the experience of an event, object, scene, and situation to its own integral fulfillment.* The connection of form with substance is thus inherent, not imposed from without. It marks the matter of an experience that is carried to consummation. (Dewey 1934: 142)

Similarly, then, in an environment spelled out by widespread functions such as the one in which we move about in our everyday lives, people relate to their own environments in the same way, understanding the latter's contents as experiential devices. They are indications, expressive experiential constructs "that speak to us", potential proximal neighborhoods. Form is what allows an objectual content to become an experiential device, a generator of experience. However, it is not the form of the object as such that renders it a device, but the form of experience as interaction.[11] There is, in fact, a cooperation between "subjectual" instances, or instances pertaining in some way to the pole of something that we could define "subjectivity", and "objectual" instances, or instances pertaining in some way to the pole of something that we could define "objective world".

A second step through which Dewey proceeds in his analysis is represented, not by chance, by the distinction between "matter-for" and "matter-in" in production.

What Dewey is describing is respectively "what one is talking about", "what is represented", "that to which the title refers", and the substance of the aesthetic in an experiential sense. In the first case what is at stake is something that can be described in various ways without being questioned or affecting the experience of which it is part. In the second case, Dewey refers to the "work of art" as such. The latter, however, is not understood as something "objective", so to speak, but rather as a device that works exactly in a certain way and that could not be expressed otherwise because it has been treated by "the artist".

> The fact that form and matter are connected in a work of art does not mean that they are identical. It signifies that in the work of art they do not offer themselves as two distinct things: the work is formed matter. But they are legitimately distinguished when reflection sets in. (Dewey 1934: 118–9)

Sometimes Dewey seems almost obsessive in his aim to clarify how form and content are related. However, this "obsession" is justified — and it cannot be stressed enough — by the fact that the previous tradition of aesthetics (which, as far as Dewey's philosophical program is concerned can be described rightfully as a philosophy of experience) was strongly dualistic and paradoxical. The paradox here is that, on the level of direct experience, we do not pose the question of form and content.

Yet, he says, from an analytical point of view, "we must have a conception of what is form generically" (Dewey 1934: 119).

---

11   On "form and process" see the seminal text Alexander (1987: 233–49).

It is precisely this passage, after having addressed the level of production (with the distinction between "matter-for" and "matter-in"), that leads the discourse back to the level of perception, of consumption, and it does so in a way that is particularly interesting for the topic at the center of the present essay. What is now introduced by Dewey is the treatment of the question of the end at which an aesthetic construct must aim, namely the relationship between function and form.

> We may get a key to this idea by starting from the fact that one idiomatic use of the word makes it equivalent with shape or figure. [...] Now shape is only an element in esthetic form; it does not constitute it. [...] For shape in relation to recognition is not limited to geometric or spatial properties. The latter play a part only as they are subordinated to *adaptation to an end*. Shapes that are not in our minds associated with any function are hard to grasp, to retain. (Dewey 1934: 119)

As far as there is a direct connection to an adaptation to an end, that is, as far as a link to use is concerned:

> up to a certain point, then shape is allied with form in its artistic sense. In both there is organization of constituent parts. In some sense the typical shape of even a utensil and tool indicates that the meaning of the whole has entered into the parts to qualify them. (Dewey 1934: 119)

At this point, the question becomes: does the relationship between form and content/substance, so explained, also help to clarify the relationship that exists between the aesthetic (generally: form as an aesthetic element) and the useful (that is, the functional content of something)?

> A good deal of intellectual effort has been expended in trying to identify efficiency for a particular end with 'beauty' or esthetic quality. But these attempts are bound to fail, fortunate as it is that in some cases the two coincide and humanly desirable as it is that they should always meet. For adaptation to a particular end is often (always in the case of complicated affairs) something perceived by

thought while esthetic effect is found directly in sense perception. (Dewey 1934: 119–20)

As Marolda (1994) has noted, what is properly at stake here is the possibility of perceiving aesthetically something in relation to a specific use, to a specific function.

Interestingly, Dewey seems to recall something we have already mentioned in our earlier discussion on Usability, User Experience and Experience Design. The separation between the kind of perception linked to the adaptation to a particular end, meant as cognitive, and the kind of perception linked to a more involving, holistic dimension of experience, meant as aesthetic, seems to refer precisely to the important shift from a cognitivist approach (as in Usability) to a more prominently aesthetic approach (as in User Experience Design). In particular, Dewey provides the example of the perception of various typologies of chairs, i.e. chairs intended for different specific uses. Even if these chairs performed their instrumental function well, but did not satisfy "at the same time the needs of the eye" (Dewey 1934: 120), they would be ugly, since while facilitating functionality they would hinder aesthetic perception. This statement by Dewey, in which the perceptual-aesthetic dimension is limited to vision, could be unsettling, especially if we consider the holistic framework in which Dewey's perspective moves. In fact, it affords an opportunity to illustrate a characteristic of Dewey's methodology of investigation. Vision, here and elsewhere in *Art as Experience*, is understood by Dewey as a *pars pro-toto*, as a perceptual area that extends itself as perception. If one does not read Dewey in this way, one runs the risk to understand his position as a reassertion of the dichotomy between form and function, and thus to misunderstand it. What Dewey does, instead, is using a label that then integrates itself into a holistic system. Visual contemplation is understood as the degree zero of the complexity of the perceptual dynamics, which is thus more articulated.

The question becomes even more relevant for our topic of inquiry when Dewey states the following:

There is no preëstablished harmony that guarantees that what satisfies one set of organs will fulfill that of all the other structures and needs that have a part in the experience, so as to bring it to completion as a complex of all elements. All we can say is that in the absence of disturbing contexts, such as production of objects for a maximum of private profit, a balance tends to be struck so that objects will be satisfactory — 'useful' in the strict sense — to the self as a whole, even though some specific efficiency be sacrificed in the process. In so far there is a tendency for dynamic shape (as distinguished from bare geometric figure) to blend with artistic form. (Dewey 1934: 120)

It seems possible to identify in this passage some indications that are coherent with those provided in the first chapter of this essay in the description of the further shift from User Experience Design to Experience Design.

The lack of "preëstablished harmony" — which seems to recall that same "Ohne Leitbild", "Without Model", that Adorno used as both the title of an essay and as part of the title of the book in which the essay on functionalism that we will address in the following chapter was included — could be referred to the fact that, although experiences are indeed to be designed in Experience Design, the interaction is anyway never fully "designable". In other words, although there are certainly some consolidated (yet surely context sensitive) principles to be followed in designing something (such as experiences) that can help in making the process as successful as possible, design(ers) can rather only "nudge" the accomplishment — or, using a Deweyan vocabulary, the consummation — of an experience, for the (human) contribution of the "user" cannot be eliminated.

In these lines Dewey seems to refer to a "principle of economy" which, when applied to design, disharmonizes experience *as a whole* (i.e. harmony is not pre-established but is struck *in the course of* experience). Why does Dewey make this point? Because he wants to clarify that, when speaking of "useful[ness] in the strict sense" he does not use such an expression in a necessarily utilitarian-capitalistic sense. Rather, he seems to refer to the meaning of the deponent Latin verb "utor (uteris, usus sum, uti)". Deponent verbs are verbs that occur in a passive voice but are translated in active voice. In them, the active–passive nexus which is so important for Dewey is strongly emphasized. Not only, the range of meanings covered by the verb "utor" is quite interesting. It includes such meanings as "to use", "to experience", "to undergo", "to enjoy", "to wear", "to consume". Usefulness in a Deweyan sense could be understood as what Dewey means by "consummation", that is, an experience which is "satisfactory [...] to the self as a whole".

As far as the relationship between form and function is concerned, this can be read as the maximum realization of form for that content, or end which is internal, or intrinsic to the work, not meant as an object but as an experience. The maximum realization of form that Dewey is referring to is the maximum realization of the experiential components as a whole ("an experience") because the relationship is "useful", and the self is, so to speak, extended. This seems to justify the passage in which Dewey maintains that "some specific efficiency be sacrificed in the process". This means that the realization of (an) experience as a complex renders "specific energies" functional with respect to the "energies of the whole". Something is sacrificed, but what counts is the overall configuration, or the overall success of the interaction, that is to say, an interaction in which we find a correspondence between the expressivity of an environment and the perceptual involvement and responsiveness of an organism to which it appeals.

This process has also been explained in terms of "abstraction"[12] (see Matteucci 2015: 27–9). Abstraction does not mean here merely reducing or simplifying something to or with pre-established or conventional solutions, but in production it concerns the

---

12   "For to perceive, a beholder must create his own experience. And his creation must include relations comparable to those which the original producer underwent. They are not the same in any literal sense. But with the perceiver, as with the artist, there must be an ordering of the elements of the whole that is in form, although not in details, the same as the process of organization the creator of the work consciously experienced. Without an act of recreation the object is not perceived as a work of art. The artist selected, simplified, clarified, abridged and condensed according to his interest. The beholder must go through these operations according to his point of view and interest. In both, an act of abstraction, that is of extraction of what is significant, takes place. In both, there is comprehension in its literal signification — that is, a gathering together of details and particulars physically scattered into an experienced whole" (Dewey 1934: 60).

management of the complexity of experience as to qualitatively enhance perceptual processes.[13] This means that its function is to intensify the naturalness of the latter, by facilitating and maximizing their overall "natural course", regardless of specific details that are directly pursued. Again, it is a matter of "coolness", both on the side of the producer and of the perceiver.[14] And, again, this "coolness" shows how challenging (i.e. in its being paradoxical) can be understanding Experience Design, as it has to thematize something which, by definition, refrains from being fully thematized: experience in its "naturality".

This discussion, in fact, makes the question of an "experiential disturbance" particularly worth of being addressed. A disturbing context implies the partialization of the overarching, overall relationship or interaction. It takes place when specific ends, special purposes are pursued. There is disturbance when action is oriented towards ends that are external, extrinsic to the experiential field. Yet, this same disturbance can also exist within the experiential field as such when something impedes flowing experiential dynamics.

Hence it can be described in terms of a polarization in a "subjectual" sense, that is, inherent in a dimension where something that we could somewhat define as "subjective" is involved and in a "objectual" sense, that is, inherent in a dimension where something that we could somewhat define as "objective" is involved. This word choice, again, derives from the need not to lose Dewey's interactive and anti-dualistic understanding of experience.

In the first case there is a subjectual "projection" of the disturbance which is oriented towards personal profit. In this sense it implies an attitude that can be defined as both economicistic and

---

13   In this framework the nexus perception–expression has also been described, following Cassirer as a double constraint of the aesthetic in "perceptualization": on the one hand art emerges within the domain of the perceptual, and on the other hand it leans towards, it tends towards the domain of the perceptual, see Matteucci (2015: 44).

14   A way to understand the ability to make something work aesthetically from the point of view of personal appearance and fashion is the question of hyper-correctism in processes of social mimetism as developed in Carnevali (2012: 171–87).

hedonistic, as it concerns an exclusively momentary dimension of pleasure. In this case we are dealing with a mere cosmetic exteriority that involves a partial usage of things, not things in their full potential. In other words, it is a detrimental and lesser form of usefulness: it is consumerism understood as ab-use, that is, as taking something and dismissing it before it is exhausted.

These are aspects that Experience Design tends to favour, to the detriment of a sustainable and balanced conception of experience. They concern the dimension of exploitation and hedonism.

In the second case there is an objectual "projection" of the disturbance that indicates the presence of dispersive elements in the environment that prevent the compagination of experience from taking place.

These are aspects that Experience Design tends instead to minimize, leaning in its extreme towards a mechanization and homogenization of experience to the detriment of an all-encompassing conception of the latter. The dimension, essential for Dewey, in which there is a complex alternation of tensions and progressions, would seem to be nullified here.

Both these cases, *if* taken in their so to speak "unsustainable–hedonistic" or "mechanical–homogeneous" extremes, are denoted by a lack of aesthetic competence. In the first case, one is unable to respond perceptually to the expressiveness of the field; in the second case, one does not create the expressive conditions that appeal to the perceptual ability to respond to it.

What is not valued in both of these cases is that tendency "to artisticity", that tendency "to blend with artistic form", that Dewey refers to in the above mentioned passage. The word "tendency" could be read in terms of qualitative potential, and its valorization in terms of activation of that potential. On the other hand, when these processes occur, also (and especially in our case) in extra-artistic areas, there is a tendency to transform experience so that it becomes "immediately recognizable" (i.e., when it takes on aesthetic form) because it holds together experientially cohesive elements in which the formal component is co-implicated with the functional one, and there are no detachable "pieces" of experience (such as a geometric form, or a stereotyped solution) as such. Form is not limited to the purpose but is also charged with other meanings.

The relationship between sense and meaning, understood as a matter of integration of form and function (or functional content), is also explained by analyzing the "moot problem of the relation of the decorative and the expressive" (Dewey 1934: 130).

> Were enjoyment simply of qualities by themselves, the decorative and the expressive would have no connection with each other, one coming from immediate sense experience and the other from relations and meanings introduced by art. Since sense itself blends with relations, the difference between the decorative and the expressive is one of emphasis. [...] The special bearing of the expressiveness of decoration on the problem of substance and form is that it proves the wrongness of the theories that isolate sense qualities. For in the degree in which decorative effect is achieved by isolation, it becomes empty embellishment, factitious ornamentation. [...] There is no need for me to go out of my way to condemn the insincerity of using adornment to conceal weakness and cover up structural defects [...]. Insincerity in art has an esthetic, not just a moral source; it is found wherever substance and form fall apart. This statement does not signify that all structurally necessary elements should be evident to perception, as some extreme 'functionalists' in architecture have insisted they should be. [...] In architecture as in painting and in poetry, raw materials are reordered through interaction with the self to make experience delightful. [...] The truth of the matter is that what is form in one connection is matter in another and vice-versa. (Dewey 1934: 132–3)

Once again, Dewey is critical of isolationist (and therefore non-immersive) theories or approaches to experience, not least in addressing the issue of decoration. This offers him the opportunity to talk about "insincerity" and "truth" in production, that is, of the ability — or otherwise — to facilitate perception in its naturalness. "Insincere" would be all that is not able to facilitate it, and "true" would be all that is inherent in and promotes such a mode of perception, even at the cost of sacrificing certain elements in the process. On the contrary, the most orthodox functionalism hypostatizes the meaning of function, and considers it as absolute, by determining and setting everything out explicitly, directly "in clear". In doing so, it does not express, but states or asserts, exactly in the terms indicated by Dewey.[15]

In other words, extremes, be they "decorative" (in a lesser sense of form) or "functional" (in a merely instrumental sense) become assertive, almost prescriptive, as they no longer perform their "inviting" task. In this sense they sterilize, arrest the expressive component.

One could say that, instead, according to a principle of indeterminacy, which is potentiality, from a specifically aesthetic point of view form and substance, form and function, depend on the manner in which we relate to whatever we are dealing with. It is not coincidental that Dewey uses the term "transferred value", which indicates a movement, the valorization of a potential through the intensification of the meaning of a context in another context.

> Not colors, not sense qualities as such, are either matter or form, but these qualities as thoroughly imbued, impregnated, with transferred value. And then they are either matter or form according to the direction of our interest. (Dewey 1934: 123)

The underlying reason for this claim is that "form" and "function", as Dewey suggests, are not to be considered as isolable or isolated elements. They are complex spectra that have internal gradations and meanings that in their "higher" ends meet and fuse and in their "lower" ends part.

---

15   "The problem at hand may be approached by drawing a distinction between expression and statement. Science states meanings; art expresses them. [...] Statement sets forth the conditions under which an experience of an object or situation may be had. It is a good, that is, effective, statement in the degree in which these conditions are stated in such a way that they can be used as *directions* by which one may arrive at the experience. [...] Expression as distinct from statement does something different from leading to an experience. It constitutes one. [...] The poem, or painting, does not operate in the dimension of correct descriptive statement but in that of experience itself. Poetry and prose, literal photograph and painting, operate in different media to distinct ends. Prose is set forth in propositions. The logic of poetry is super-propositional even when it uses what are, grammatically speaking, propositions. The latter have intent; art is an immediate realization of intent" (Dewey 1934: 91).

The spectrum of the meaning of form ranges from shape (as detached) to configuration (as something which is "fully rounded"). The spectrum of the meaning of function ranges from mechanism (for want of a better term) to consummation (as something which is "satisfactory to the self as a whole"). Here a sort of equivalence applies: the more the function is consummation, the more it is integrated with the configuration; the more the function is mechanism, the more it is separated from the shape. When there is shape and mechanism, form and function part from and contrast with each other; when there is the extreme of the shape, it is at the expense of the mechanism: the mechanism is sacrificed for the shape and the aestheticist forms of embellishment, a so-called sugar coating of experience, prevail; when there is pure mechanism, the shape is sacrificed and the same orthodox functionalism as that promoted by Adolf Loos, for instance, in terms of a mechanical functionalism, prevails (see Fig. 1).

To provide a summary of the kind of functionality that stems out of Dewey's conception of form we may speak in one case of a "instrumental/operational functionality" — "operationality" to be understood as the capacity to function properly and to accomplish a certain task; in the other case we may speak instead of a "working/operative functionality" — "operativity" to be understood as the capacity of having force in a specific context, of being meaningful. The former is aimed at the achievement of an external purpose. In this case, shape is such with respect to a purpose that is external and therefore detachable from the whole. It is obtained as a result of an operational process. On the contrary, as far as operativity is concerned the purpose is internal (it is hyper-functional; it concerns a hyper-consummatory process). The configuration results as the way of configuring operativity in the process as such, and therefore it is more innervated. It emerges within operativity itself.[16]

---

16 For a development of the difference between operationality and operativity, understood from the point of view of the relationship between aesthetics and economics, see Iannilli (2019b).

2.4. *"We Can Do It!"*

Interestingly, in this same chapter of *Art as Experience* Dewey addresses even more explicitly the question of design, starting from its etymology:

> It is significant that the word 'design' has a double meaning. It signifies purpose and it signifies arrangement, mode of composition. [...] In both cases, there is an ordered relation of many constituent elements. (Dewey 1934: 121)

Yet, according to Dewey, an ordered relation is not enough, but what makes the difference is the modality with which these parts are held and perceived together.

> The characteristic of artistic design is the intimacy of the relations that hold the parts together. [The] interfusion of all properties of the medium is necessary if the object in question is to serve the whole creature in his unified vitality. (Dewey 1934: 121, 122)

This idea of "intimacy" and "interfusion" seems to strengthen the conception of Experience Design that we have tried to put forward so far, that is, as concerning a gratifying and densely personal, meaningful space that the self inhabits.

Design is experiential ("artistic") when it is not felt to be superimposed, when there is no specialized, but inclusive purpose: when it "feels good". As far as Experience Design is concerned, when we speak of an end or of purposefulness from an aesthetic viewpoint, it always concerns an end, a purposefulness which is internal and never external as respects experience itself. There is a sort of "closure" — not in a detrimental and lesser sense — of the aesthetic, that is to say there is a holistic, immersive and focused structuration of generic experience which hence becomes "an" experience. There is not something that stands out by itself, but the significance, the meaningfulness of the experience concerns the interaction in its "fused unity". This also means that, although there is a strong component of construction of experience, users are not exclusively passive "participants" in someone else's design. Actually, "things don't work" if there is not a first-hand experience of a user (i.e. the "immediacy of esthetic experience" that Dewey defines as a true and proper "esthetic necessity", see Dewey 1934: 123).

> [Industrial] objects take on esthetic form [...] when the material is so arranged and adapted that it serves immediately the enrichment of the immediate experience of the one whose attentive perception is directed to. [...] Only a twisted and aborted logic can hold that because something is mediated, it cannot, therefore, be immediately experienced (Dewey 1934: 121, 125).

By this Dewey not only shows that, in fact, the hiatus between artistic and aesthetic (in the sense of a nexus between expression and perception, doing and undergoing in which what is "cultivated" and what is "natural" blend together) does not subsist, but also shows that in contexts which are highly saturated, that is, highly mediated, such as those in which Experience Design operates, it is possible to acquire and carry out competence and reactivity, i.e. attentive perception in perceptually grasping the meaningfulness expressed by that with which we interact. And it is so because:

> meanings [have] their source in past experience [...] and the organism which responds in production of the experienced object [...] carries past experiences in itself not by conscious memory but by direct charge. (Dewey 1934: 127–8)

Dewey seems to describe at least three different modes of processing and managing past experienced material, as the following quotations suggest:

> In purely automatic action, past material is subordinated to the extent of *not appearing at all in consciousness* [emphasis added]. (Dewey 1934: 128)

This seems to recall something that Larry Hickman (2001: 17) has described as concerning a "technical" dimension of experience, i.e. something "generally and for the most part habitual. It is non-cognitive and non-inferential".

In other cases, *material of the past comes to consciousness* but is consciously employed as an instrument to deal with some present problem and difficulty. It is kept down as *to serve some special end*. If the experience is predominatingly one of investigation, it has the status of offering evidence or of suggesting hypotheses; if 'practical' of furnishing cues to present action [emphases added]. (Dewey 1934: 128)

This seems to recall something that Larry Hickman (2001: 17) has defined as concerning a "technological" dimension of experience, i.e. something generally pertaining to a "cognitive or deliberate inferential activity. It intervenes when someone wants to address some perceived problem".

However, these two dimensions are not to be understood as dichotomous or mutually exclusive. Actually, they cooperate and dynamically contribute to the subsistence of the other.

> Cognition that involves the use of tools and artifacts that are relatively external to the organism is what I have termed 'technology'. But once technological work has been done, that is, once problematic situations have been resolved with the help of those tools and artifacts, their solutions tend to be habitualized or routinized. Techniques are then stored as habits and used as needed. When habitualized techniques are applied to problematic situations but fail to resolve them, then more technology — more deliberate inquiry into techniques — is called for. (Hickman 2001: 23)

Similarly, what acts operatively in common experience becomes to a certain extent thematic and cognitive: it is a matter of labeling explicitly certain functions and making them available. The point is that we should be able to see all this as an interweaving and not as a dichotomy.

However, if it is true that it is our relationship with the past that characterizes our competences in dealing with the present, then we could sketch a definition of the kind of competence implied by these first two cases. The first one could be defined as a "technical competence" inhering in a dimension of "knowing-how" (i.e. an operative dimension). It concerns a procedure that, when applied, allows accomplishing a certain task, to reach a certain goal, namely a practical competence. The second one could be defined as a "technological competence" inhering in a dimension of "knowing-that" (i.e. a thematic dimension). It concerns a scientific inquiry, it is a scientific knowledge. The first one has to do with a "denser" level, as a "technique" sometimes can only be learned or taught by doing, rather than being cognitively understood. The second one has to do with an epistemic knowledge that is then applied, also through specific techniques on which it relies; it implies the usage of a theoretical knowledge, which can be quantified.

As far as Experience Design is concerned the one in charge of the technological competence is the designer. Yet, when one designs experiences, it is more than just dealing with one's own scientific competence. The more a user needs to know how to "use" something, that is, a technique to make a specific technology work, the least the design is successful. As we have seen, the developments occurred in HCI emblematically show how from the usage of the first machines, until third wave HCI, to which Experience Design belongs, a progressive emancipation of the user from technological and technical competences has taken place. It is now more than ever a matter of seamless, flowing interaction. In other terms, interaction no longer concerns an experience of something, as something which is opposed to us, and that we need to cognitively determine in order to accomplish a task, but it concerns an experience with something, as something we need and that needs us in order to be deemed "working". These developments, as we have seen in the first chapter, are linked to the increasing centrality of the aesthetic component in design that also corresponds to the increasing centrality of the role of the "user".

Interestingly, a third dimension is described by Dewey, and it has chiefly to do with aesthetic experience:

> In esthetic experience, on the contrary, *the material of the past neither fills attention, as in recollection, nor is subordinated to a special purpose.* There is indeed a restriction imposed upon what comes. But it is that of contribution to the immediate matter of an experience now had. The material is not employed as a bridge to some further experience, but as an increase and individualization of present experience. The scope of a work of art is measured by the number and variety of elements coming from past experiences

that are *organically absorbed* into the perception had here and now [emphases added]. (Dewey 1934: 128)

Let's unpack this passage: in aesthetic experience there is no predominance of the material of the past in the current "attentive perception" (otherwise it would be mere recollection, a glimpse, while perception takes time, it is a process)[17] nor is it subordinated to a special purpose. Yet, there is a link with the future, not as a mere instrumental projection (as the purpose would be external), but as a richer way of dealing with current experience while envisaging (or imagining) and increasing its potential. This can and should also be read in terms of an ability to take care, to *mind*, using a Deweyan concept, both about the past (i.e. our heritage), the present (i.e. our current life conditions) and the future (i.e. how we think, or imagine, things should and will be) of our interactions with the environment.

It is an ability to keep things together organically while shifting between various levels, an ability to make generic experience "an" individualized experience. It is an aesthetic competence.

As compared to the other two kinds of experiences, it could be said that it shares with the first one the embodiment, the absorption of something which is carried out operatively, and which is not cognitively thematized, as is the case with technological competence. It can be said that both technical and aesthetic competence imply a "knowing-how" rather than a technological "knowing-that".

Is there any difference between them? What makes one aesthetic and the other technical?

The kind of relationship that one has in the present with the past defines, as we have seen, the types of competence involved in experience. Competence, the know-how, is more or less aesthetic depending on how the past is assimilated and re-issued into the world. One may even say that competence has to do with the style with which one perceives. It is a style of perception which, as such,

---

17   "What is true of original production is true of appreciative perception. We speak of perception *and* its object. But perception and *its* object are built up and completed in one and the same continuing operation" (Dewey 1934: 181).

also implies a kind of creativity that is not necessarily productive, but also denotes the capacity to manage a particular situation by "dwelling in it", or inhabiting it, in the best and most gratifying way possible (in the richest and fullest sense of the word as consummation).[18] It cannot be stressed enough, though, that the temporal dimension of experience and competence in and with experience in Dewey is not limited to the relationship between past and present. It concerns a rich link between past–present– future. The imaginative component plays a great role in Dewey's philosophical project also in this sense. Actually, as the following quotations indicate, it denotes a true and proper competence using terms and emphasizing modalities that we have already linked to a "truly" aesthetic dimension. Dewey describes it as "a warm and intimate taking in of the full scope of a situation" (Dewey 1916: 244), and discerns it from the "imaginary" by applying a temporal criterion: "Time is the test that discriminates the imaginative from the imaginary. The latter passes because it is arbitrary. The imaginative endures because, while at first strange with respect to us, it is enduringly familiar with respect to the nature of things" (Dewey 1934: 274).

However, competence for Dewey is something that has different degrees of realization, of consciousness, of development, and these degrees or levels are not dichotomous but related. What they have in common is the fact that the experientiality of form remains central, if not even fundamental. Competence concerns the more or less marked abilities to adequately manage forms with respect to a medium, that is to say to functionalize a form (be it a researcher's, an artist's, a craftsman's, a designer's, a user's).

Much of what is a simple "operative how" of experience, in a successful Experience Design becomes a "thematic what" which, however, feeds on the operativity of the how and does not go contrary to, or cancel, the operativity of the how, because if it were to be solved only in a technical or technological manual it

---

18   In this respect it is worth quoting again the following passage in which Dewey notes how "Sometimes, the effect is to separate [the artistic and the esthetic] from each other, to regard art as something superimposed upon esthetic material, or, upon the other side, to an assumption that, since art is a process of creation, perception and enjoyment of it have nothing in common with the creative act" (Dewey 1934: 53).

would lose the capacity of impacting experience. The peculiarity of the specialized and professional technical and technological competences of the designers is that they render thematic what can be thematized without, however, losing the effect of operativity. They solve, measure or generalize only partially the operativity of experience, whose quality and particularity they must respect, because otherwise they would be prescriptive. Design and in particular Experience Design, as we have seen, does not only concern measurements or quantifying activities. Quite the opposite: through quantification it must produce the effect of operativity, even if it can be very thematized. It is something that lies on a threshold between thematization and intensification (see Fig. 2). It is a question of coolness, a practice of "nudging" meant as an invitation to do something. In this sense, symmetrically, when a user acquires a certain aesthetic competence, or know-how, designed configurations, or experiential frameworks, that are certainly pre-established and made available, provided (or sometimes aggressively imposed, that's undeniable) by design, are not perceived as predetermined empirical-factual contents as such but become conditions for operativity, or experiential modalities that must be implemented according to the perceptual and expressive potential of the interaction with the environment.

Hence, to answer our previous question, when we speak of "techniques", we speak of something that (although always learnable and improvable) tends to be quite specialistic, consolidated, as it generally implies the conventional application of models and solutions. When we speak of the aesthetic, as we have seen, we speak of a dense complex of experience which is deeply personal, situational, emotional, felt and gratifying, which cannot be tamed as such, as it is carried out uniquely in the overall interaction between a human being and an environment — to the extent that some specific efficiency may be sacrificed in the process. This conception of Experience Design, understood also with the help of John Dewey, has hence corroborated the non-dichotomous relationship between form and function that we put forward already in the first chapter of this essay. It has to do precisely with the same cross-layering of levels that also Dewey has emphasized. It cannot be reduced to a mere rational efficacy in the design and accomplishment of a task (function), nor to a mere emotional and pleasurable design and enjoyment of shapes, textures, colors or other sensual elements (form). It concerns a deep cooperation of various energies. When it becomes "an" experience, these energies cannot be discerned as such.

The following passage summarizes well the whole point:

> [The elements coming from past experiences] give [the work of art] its body and its suggestiveness. They often come from sources too obscure to be identified in any conscious memorial way, and thus they create the aura and the penumbra in which a work of art swims. (Dewey 1934: 128)

In these few lines Dewey brings together the concreteness (i.e. the body) and the nudge-like attitude (the suggestiveness) of a working (experiential) aesthetic device (the work of art). Not only it exists specifically within an interaction between the self and the common world, but it actually invites to an interaction. Moreover, Dewey manages to visually render the way in which temporal and spatial dimensions are to be understood in this interaction. Past, present and future are held together by an interplay of light and shadow (or of aura and penumbra): the experiential field is not neutral, it is thickly constellated by elements that when brightened, also to the point they get saturated, necessarily cast a shadow somewhere else. And it is precisely in this thick substance, that the working (experiential) aesthetic device happily flows, floats and is immersed (it swims there).

Finally, although Dewey finds that it has been "hardened" or "hypostatized" by philosophy as an essence, he nevertheless maintains that the concept of beauty could still describe this fully rounded interpenetration of substance and form, of function and form. "It is properly an emotional term" (Dewey 1934: 135), that is to say, it qualifies the interaction, the experience as consummated, where organism and environment correspond to each other. It is our feeling ourselves part of that environment, it is feeling ourselves belonging to, immersed, fitting in that interaction:

> Beauty is the response to that which to reflection is the consummated movement of matter integrated through its inner relations into a single qualitative whole. (Dewey 1934: 135)

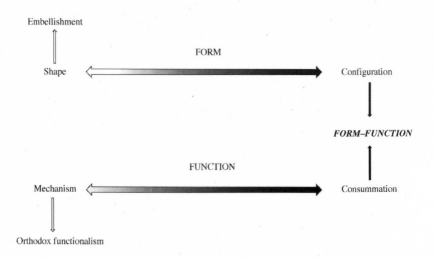

Fig. 1

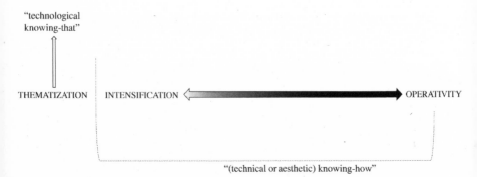

Fig. 2

3.
THEODOR W. ADORNO:
FUNCTION AS FORM

3.1. *Adorno's Diagnosis About Beauty*

This chapter turns to Theodor W. Adorno and his perspective on the concept of function, in order to delve deeper into some of the questions raised in the first chapter concerning the consequences of Experience Design and its aesthetics. In so doing, the present chapter points to the topicality of Adorno's perspective, despite the fact that this latter might appear at first sight hardly compatible with the so far outlined features of the phenomenon here under investigation.

A good starting point for such an investigation could be a passage from Adorno's work in which he delivers a diagnosis that is something of a curve-ball. The passage wrong-foots indeed the reader who takes Adorno's aesthetic accounts canonically. According to a certain canonical interpretive standard, Adorno is in fact an unwearying and melancholic supporter of the Great autonomous art, in other words, the type of absolute art that has been supposedly contaminated, relativized, therefore expelled from the current reality, functionalized, and commodified. Surprisingly, Adorno claims instead that:

> Aesthetics becomes a practical necessity once it becomes clear that concepts like usefulness and uselessness in art, like the separation of autonomous and purpose-oriented art, imagination and ornament, must once again be discussed before the artist can act positively or negatively according to such categories. [...] Beauty today can have no other measure except the depth to which a work resolves contradictions. A work must cut through the contradictions and overcome them, not by covering them up, but by pursuing

them. Mere formal beauty, whatever that might be, is empty and meaningless; the beauty of its content is lost in the preartistic sensual pleasure of the observer. Beauty is either the resultant of force vectors or it is nothing at all. A modified aesthetics would outline its own object with increasing clarity as it would begin to feel more intensely the need to investigate it. Unlike traditional aesthetics, it would not necessarily view the concept of art as its given correlate. Aesthetic thought today must surpass art by thinking art. It would thereby surpass the current opposition of purposeful and purpose-free, under which the producer must suffer as much as the observer. (Adorno 1966: 17)

These are the concluding remarks of Adorno's essay "Functionalism Today", published in 1966, which stems from Adorno's guest conference speech at the *Deutscher Werkbund* the previous year.

These few lines sum up the complex argument of the essay, pointing to how some polarizations of the experiential field (i.e., useful–useless; superfluous–necessary; autonomy–heteronomy; imagination–handicraft; ornament–function; including also desire–need; etc.) must be handled from a specifically aesthetic point of view. It is significant that these remarks ensue from openly detecting a lack of standards, laws, purposes, categories of definition, that is to say, the lack of *Maß* and, more generally, of models of reference — hence the title of the first edition of the volume including this essay: *Ohne Leitbild. Parva Aesthetica* — to be affirmatively applied to reality according to a merely abstract, "top-down", model. The non-negligible points of convergence between Adorno and Dewey in this respect might come as a surprise. The surprise might be however mitigated if one reads Adorno's remark full of admiration for Dewey's work in *Aesthetic Theory* ("the unique and truly free John Dewey", Adorno 1970: 335) — something already atypical for an advocate of the Critical Theory, given the well-known disagreements and controversies between critical theorists and pragmatists. The first point of convergence can be found precisely in the way in which both Adorno and Dewey stress the absence of pre-defined models, which can be read, as both authors do, as the absence of a "pre-established harmony", which also means that "superimposed" layers of experience in aesthetic production and perception are a mistake.

Adorno describes the polarizations as tendencies simultaneously at work, *in re*, despite the fact that they are in contradiction with one another within the experiential field understood as aesthetic field. It is not a coincidence that Adorno speaks of a "practical necessity" justifying the peculiar perspective he embraces while dealing with the topics and issues here under investigation. This means that he advocates an aesthetics which takes into account the current situation and does justice to the tendencies that innervate it. Although reciprocally incongruent, these are historical tendencies, and as such they must be assessed and not mystified or ideologically removed. To this aim, according to Adorno, aesthetics must undergo a radical self-criticism, coming to terms thereby both with the contradictions of the present reality and with the contradictions of the traditional set of categories applied to the investigation of its defining phenomena. As the following quote clarifies, Adorno is adamant that: "If it [*scil.*: aesthetics] continued academically without the most ruthless self-criticism, it would already be condemned" [English translation modified, as in the original version Adorno states: "Machte sie akademisch weiter ohne die rücksichtsloseste Selbstkritik, so wäre sie schon verurteilt"] (Adorno 1966: 17).

Within this context, aesthetics is defined by Adorno mainly in reference to the concept of beauty. This is also the notion — notwithstanding the issue ensuing from its hypostatization in philosophical theory — Dewey refers to as he describes the quality of the aesthetic experience he investigates. Beauty, in both instances, is neither reduced to its formal level as something purely external, nor to its contents (or functions). Beauty is also not mere harmony, nor is it the harmonization of different instances, but it is such insofar as it handles the polarizations at work without trying to solve, conciliate, or so to speak "dumbing down" the relation among them and between them and the other vectors in the field. On the contrary, beauty indulges in contradictions, emphasizes the conflicts that innervate it and "dwells in them", inhabits them.[1]

---

1   Such "being compromised" with material reality is well explained in Adorno's reading of the relationship between art and fashion. Such

This dwelling, or better, this ability to dwell in, or inhabiting, a "parallelogram of forces" entails the retrieval of a dimension of aesthetics which goes beyond the obvious correlation with artisticity, or at least is not limited to it, exactly as it is not limited within the perimeter of *simple* contradiction between "what is purposeful and what is purpose-free". The field investigated by this "modified aesthetics" is then defined by the range of phenomena sharing the "obscure secret" (Adorno 1966: 16) of aestheticization. And it should also be made clear that Adorno's proposal appeals to producers as well as to users to take a share in the management of the *complex* contradiction between the several polarities at play. Producers and users are equal vectors of the aesthetic field, and as such should perform the same radical self-criticism Adorno deems necessary for any aesthetics that wants to be "responsible", most of all because "responsive", that is to say, capable of *responding* to the needs of the life context. In this regard, in his essay on functionalism, Adorno expresses his wish for a useful that is "a 'happy' [*glückliche*] use, a contact with things beyond the antithesis between use and

---

a relationship is necessary for the artwork in order to contrast the commodification in place in current reality, by greatly becoming itself a commodity, following fashion's example (see Matteucci 2009: 97–8). Adorno maintains that: "In the face of the obvious dependency of fashion on the profit motive and its embeddedness in capitalist industry — which, for instance in the art market , which finances painters but overtly or covertly demands in exchange that they furnish whatever style of work the market expects of them, extends into so-called artistic fashions and directly undermines autonomy-fashion in art is no less corruptible than the zeal of ideological art agents who transform every apology into advertisement. What makes it worth salvaging, however, is that though it hardly denies its complicity with the profit system, it is itself disdained by that system. By suspending aesthetic values such as those of inwardness, timelessness, and profundity, fashion makes it possible to recognize the degree to which the relation of art to these qualities, which are by no means above suspicion, has become a pretext. Fashion is art's permanent confession that it is not what it claims to be. For its indiscreet betrayals fashion is as hated as it is a powerful force in the system; its double character is a blatant symptom of its antinomy. [...] If it is not to betray itself, art must resist fashion, but it must also innervate fashion in order not to make itself blind to the world, to its own substance. [...] Through fashion, art sleeps with what it must renounce and from this draws the strength that otherwise must atrophy under the renunciation on which art is predicated" (Adorno 1970: 316–7).

uselessness" (Adorno 1966: 16). Although Adorno's viewpoint is that of a producer speaking to an audience of "producers", these important remarks, placed emphatically at the end of the essay, point beyond this perspective. A key position is given — here, as in Dewey — to the issue of overcoming the hiatus between producer and user, in the direction of an increasing focus on the importance of the competence enacted each time by individuals who come in contact with experiential materials to be managed. More than that, Adorno hopes for the overcoming of the antithesis between what is useful and what is not in the — Dewey echoing — direction of a "happy" human promotion.

At variance with what we might expect based on certain interpretive clichés usually attached to his work, the peculiar consequences of Adorno's diagnosis have been already anticipated. Adorno's position turns out to be very different from that of an uncompromising supporter of a straight equivalence between the aesthetic and autonomous art as such. His diagnosis appears sufficiently supported by a conceptually rich argument, so far only briefly outlined starting from the first long quotation. Its validity though is still to be proven. To this aim, his prognostic abilities will be tested against the most recent configuration of the issue to which Adorno devotes himself in his lecture from 1965, that is to say, the issue of design as currently understood in terms of Experience Design. What is at stake here is not a critical analysis of the essay, which would daringly claim that Adorno might have formulated an aesthetics of Experience Design *ante litteram*. What will be attempted is instead not only to show a different side of Adorno, thanks to the testing of his diagnosis, but also to show to what extent his inquiry on the transformation of the concept of function provides a suitable theoretical grid to see under a new light the issues that make today the core of some phenomena of aestheticization, namely Experience Design.

3.2. *Experience Between Construction and Function*

As previously anticipated, the type of functionality conveyed by Experience Design can be rightfully qualified by means of the prefix "hyper-", as to indicate a level of functionalization of the experience, which does not require any reference to a function, or purpose, external to the experience itself, but which rather coincides with its very configuration, or form. With regard to Experience Design, the conceptual couple "form–function", which historically has been understood either disjunctively, that is dichotomously as "either form or function", or as mere juxtaposition in the sense of "form and, besides, function", is here taken in the terms of a close relationality meaning "form as sedimentation of function and vice-versa".

The issue of function, clearly lying at the core of the problematic definition of the very notion of Experience Design, is directly thematized by Adorno in at least two occasions: the already mentioned essay from 1966, "Functionalism Today", and, in a densely synthetic form, in a section of *Aesthetic Theory* which in the German version is titled "Dialectics of Functionalism" (Adorno 1970: 60–1), which confirms *de facto* the arguments of the previous contribution. It is worth remarking that also other sections of his posthumous masterpiece retrieve many of the topics he deals with in "Functionalism Today". These are after all the key notions of his inquiries — from mimesis, construction, rationality and expression to style, through purposiveness, the aesthetics of form and content, handicraft, imagination, up to the intertwining of natural beauty and artistic beauty.

The relation between the so-called fine arts and the applied arts is the topic chosen by Adorno for his 1965 speech delivered to an audience of expert technicians gathered at the *Deutscher Werkbund*. This is not a random choice. While for a more detailed account on the historical context one should refer the reader at least to Betts (2007) and Katz (2019), as well as to Benjamin (2000) and Sherer (2014), it will suffice to remark here that, moved by pedagogical inspirations — the topic of the 1965 conference was precisely education and design — the *Werkbund* was founded at the beginning of the twentieth century with the intention to contain the typical *Jugendstil* drifting in design towards decoration and ornament, and promote instead, in varying degrees and on varying grounds according to the inclinations of the president in office, more technocratic ideals connected to progress and efficiency. It is also worth remarking that, as Adorno was writing his speech, pop culture had reached global success, and more playful, obsolescent, superficial, and "useless" aspects of experience had been thereby emphasized, effectively unhinging uncompromising functionality from its central position in design (see at least Hamilton 1960). As far as design theory is concerned, it would be useful to point out that the Ulm School in Germany (see at least Maldonado and Bonsiepe 1964) opposed the pop conception of design in those years. The Ulm School was centered on the rational-critical furtherment of a social and technical function of design, while the pop conception of design, running parallel to the borderline between Abstract Expressionism and Pop Art, emphasized a dimension of playfulness, consumption and ornament for their own sake.

While talking about the issue of design, Adorno mainly relies on two key notions: "construction" and "function". As to the first, reference is made to constructing as to the ability to put together and organize materials around a purpose; as to the second, attention is given to the type of relation between materials and purposes, that is to say, how given materials are functional to a given purpose. What should be made clear is that Adorno sets out to retrieve a meaning of construction and function inherently immanent in the aesthetic field.

In so doing, he has at least two critical targets. The first one is the founding father of functionalism, the Austrian architect Adolf Loos. This latter maintained that progress necessarily implies the suppression of ornaments in favour of what is functional. Functionality was then assumed in this context almost as an ethical goal. As peremptorily claimed by Loos himself:

> The enormous damage and devastation caused in aesthetic development by the revival of ornament would be easily made light of, for no one, not even the power of the state, can halt mankind's evolution. It can only be delayed. We can wait. But it is a crime against the national economy that it should result in a waste of human labour, money and material. Time cannot make good this damage [...] not only is ornament produced by criminals but also a crime is committed through the fact that ornament inflict serious injury on people's health, on the national budget and hence on cultural evolution. (Loos 1908: 21)[2]

---

2   See Long (1997) for a reconstruction of the controversial genealogy of Loos' essay. For a contemporary take on the topic see Foster (2002).

Loos embodies, according to Adorno, the bourgeois sense for practicality which has removed any symbolic, expressive — even erotic — and therefore aesthetic element from experience. Said removal — at least in its attempt — includes, for instance, also irrational and stylistic elements. One should talk here of an attempt, since, as far as irrationality is concerned, Adorno famously remarks that moments of irrationality survive in full-blown rationality ("progress and regression are entwined", Adorno 1970: 61), as they are even necessary to its functioning, and as such one must take them into account and learn how to manage them. As to a particular example, he likes to refer to advertisement, in whose omnipresence "[there is] a self-mocking contradiction [...] by its measure of material appropriateness" (Adorno 1966: 8), being at the same time "purposeful for profit" (Adorno 1966: 8). With regard to elements of style, Adorno points out that, while attempting to reduce the object to pure function, Loos' orthodox functionalism can but achieve a stylizing effect, since

> there is a factor of expression in every object. Any special relegation of this factor to art alone would be an oversimplification. It cannot be separated from objects of use. Thus, even when these objects lack expression, they must pay tribute to it by attempting to avoid it. [...] The absolute rejection of style [*unconsciously*] becomes style. (Adorno 1966: 8–9)

The same distinction between expression and assertion, already surfaced in Dewey, seems here to forcibly come again to the fore, convincingly summed up by the following, peremptory claim by Adorno: "the literal is barbaric" (Adorno 1970: 61). This is a definition that goes beyond a mere taste judgment. Like Dewey, Adorno underlines the close connection between this concept, shaped by an instrumental rationality, and a social system that, through the repression of elements ideologically and conveniently considered "ornamental", devalues the human being as such, reducing her/him to a mere economic function in production and consumption. Precisely for this reason Adorno highlights the subordination of Loos' own conception to the economic rationality of capitalism.

Against this, with these examples, among the many possible ones, Adorno wishes to show that, whenever we deal with what pertains to functionality and what pertains to ornamentalism, we plunge into the antinomic relations of two instances equally at play that precisely in their polar tension yield a plastic dialectical image of the integral human reality in its radical historicity. In this regard, "function" and "ornament" become historical concepts, indicating, that is, what acquires value or becomes superfluous, according to the particular polarization of the energy field of action — with all its vectors, including social ones.

Without the shadow of a doubt, however, both Adorno and Loos revile applied arts as such, since based on their very notion, on the one hand "objects of use suffer injustice as soon as they are mixed with what is not required by their use" [English translation modified, as Adorno in the original text stated that "den Gebrauchsdingen widerfährt Unrecht, sobald man sie mit dem versetzt, was nicht von ihrem Gebrauch gefordert ist"] (Adorno 1966: 6), and on the other hand art, and more in general the whole aesthetic device, is wronged, as soon as it is bent to purposes that are extrinsic to its field of forces. For his part, though, by making the principle of function an absolute, unilaterally prominent principle, Loos advocates an a-dialectical, that is, non-material, non-historical concept of beauty. And a so formulated idea of beauty becomes an easy target for Adorno's criticism. Equally criticized are at the same time also those forms — and lifestyles, i.e. aestheticism[3] — which are purely ornamental and have made of their distance from any form of practicality a defining feature and an identity strategy. On the whole, what Adorno stigmatizes is therefore an ideological approach to handling the two aspects, the functional and the ornamental, on the basis of which the amplifying of the one implies the reduction and sclerotization of the other. This approach reinforces a form of relation that remains unproductively dichotomous, at best a mere hybridization. On the contrary, as previously mentioned, Adorno's proposal for a "responsible" aesthetics entails taking charge of apparently contradictory elements, which display — or have displayed — the historical needs of a given context, and therefore valorizing their potential in terms of sedimented sense.

---

3   See Johnson (1969).

Adorno's second critical target is here Kant. While engaging with him, Adorno seems to aim to retrieve the topic of purposiveness (*Zweckmäßigkeit*) without any (determinate) end, as well as that of lawfulness (*Gesetzmäßigkeit*) without any (determinate) law, and at the same time overturn the perspective applied to them. Both topics are, according to Adorno, ways to express a form of functionality that is more than simply achieving a purpose external to the materials. This retrieval is possible, however, only by way of radicalization, in other words, only provided that these topics are understood beyond the Kantian context of the interplay between the faculties of the transcendental subject and according to the context of the internal dynamics of any effectual aesthetic device.

This is so inasmuch as Adorno defines the aesthetic as a rigorous construction configured according to the rules imposed by the materials and with full respect of their historicity. As we read close to the conclusion of the 1960 essay *Ohne Leitbild* ("Without Model"), with an interesting reference precisely to the themes here investigated through the conceptual couple at the core of the *Deutscher Werkbund, Sachlichkeit und Zweckform*:

> The constraint, which in vain is called into question by moving from the worldview, lies rather in the material with which the artist must work. It is the hard to overrate merit of the movements that have become known under the label *Sachlichkeit und Zweckform* to have recognized it. In the material, however, history is sedimented. Only those who are able to distinguish what has matured historically and what is irrevocably obsolete in the material itself will produce by doing justice to the latter. This is apparent to artists every time they avoid colours, forms, sounds that would indeed be possible as natural matter, but which by historical associations are in contrast with the specific sense of what they should be doing at that precise moment. This is just a different way of saying that the material does not consist of original abstract, atomic elements, which in themselves would be completely devoid of intention and of which the artistic intentions could take possession as they please, but already in itself brings intentions near to the work. It succeeds in absorbing them within its own connection while it understands them, adheres to them and thereby modifies them.[4]

---

4   This is our translation of a passage that can be found in Adorno (1977: 300).

Said construction is however never achieved in view of an external goal, but rather in order to maximize the internal energies of the aesthetic field itself. As such Adorno defines it as a "monad", but a very peculiar one. It is close in itself and rigorously conform to its immanent logic — which, as previously argued, can be said hyper-functional — but it is also the mirroring of the society in place — which it resembles precisely due to its project of extreme functionalization (see Desideri, Matteucci 2009: xxvii). In so doing, it is simultaneously autonomous and heteronomous; it reaches thereby beyond any ideological principle and moves according to a logic which places value on the antinomy: simultaneously friction point (an "absolute commodity") and expression (a "commodity among commodities") of social relations. This peculiar account on the monad, evoking the profile of a "fully rounded", "differentiated" entity, immediately echoes the idea of inhabited, personal and situated space, which has been defined above, in previous chapters, as "someone's everyday", aesthetic niche, or "an" experience.

> The degree to which aesthetic unity is itself a function of multiplicity is evident in works that out of abstract enmity to unity seek to dissolve themselves into the multiplicitous, to renounce that whereby the differentiated becomes something differentiated in the first place. Works that are absolutely in flux, whose plurality is without reference to unity, thereby become undifferentiated, monotonous, and indifferent. (Adorno 1970: 191)

Like Dewey, also Adorno sees in the work of art the *exemplary* but not *exclusive* embodiment of the above described dynamics. This is why whenever in the following quotations also from *Aesthetic Theory* — and especially in the next particularly emblematic one — one reads the word "artwork" one could read also, or even instead, "aesthetic device". All the more so in the light of the outlined considerations on the overcoming of the opposition between useful and useless art.

> Speculation all too easily falls prey to the idea of a harmony between society and artworks that has been preestablished by the world spirit. But theory must not capitulate to that relationship. The process that transpires in artworks and is brought to a standstill in them, is to be conceived as the same social process in which the

artworks are embedded; according to Leibniz's formulation, they represent this process windowlessly. The elements of an artwork acquire their configuration as a whole in obedience to immanent laws that are related to those of the society external to it. Social forces of production, as well as relations of production, return in artworks as mere forms divested of their facticity because artistic labor is social labor; moreover, they are always the product of this labor. [...] If artworks are in fact absolute commodities in that they are a social product that has rejected every semblance of existing for society, a semblance to which commodities otherwise urgently cling, the determining relation of production, the commodity form, enters the artwork equally with the social force of production and the antagonism between the two. The absolute commodity would be free of the ideology inherent in the commodity form, which pretends to exist for-another, whereas ironically it is something merely for-itself: It exists for those who hold power. This reversal of ideology into truth is a reversal of aesthetic content, and not immediately a reversal of the attitude of art to society. Even the absolute commodity remains salable and has become a 'natural monopoly'. (Adorno 1970: 236)

In his 1966 essay, however, Adorno not only offers the definition of key elements to an aesthetic theory — as, for instance, as previously mentioned, what the task of an aesthetic theory is and what beauty is — but he also defines, *ex negativo*, the aesthetic:

Nothing exists as an aesthetic object in itself, but only within the field of tension of such sublimation. Therefore there is no chemically pure purposefulness set up as the opposite of the purpose-free aesthetic. (Adorno 1966: 7)

In other words, just like it is not possible to peremptorily and affirmatively define the aesthetic — which can only be grasped *in re* in its unfolding as sublimation, which is the same as purposiveness (or purposefulness) without an end — it is also not possible conversely to think that pure practicality exists. Even when one has the intention to perform an action aimed at a determinate purpose, and the purpose of the action is its content, that is, "the what" one is after — which is quantitatively measurable — a qualitatively dense modal component is nevertheless there. And, while guiding to an extent the action, this modal component is both undeterminable as such and irreducible.

What Experience Design and Adorno's perspective on function basically share from a specifically aesthetic viewpoint is the aim to make functions available which remain immanent in the experience itself and in the configuration of its field. From this starting point a parallel path can be outlined establishing a dialogue between this recent aestheticized phenomenon and Adorno's account on design.

3.3. *An Almost Adornian Move: from Objects (to Users) to Experience*

The already mentioned (see chapter 1) progressive but crucial miniaturization, if not dematerialization, proliferation and embodiment of products in everyday practices, in other words, the shift from the design of objects to the design of experiences which has taken place approximately in the last four decades, seems to conveniently lend itself to an interpretation based on Adorno's terms. The context of reference would therefore no longer be a theory of aesthetic experience where matter takes center stage as "objective" construction on which the subject is supposed to bestow meaning, but rather a theory of aesthetic experience which brings to the fore the sense potential historically sedimented in the *material,* this latter being understood as something pervaded by field dynamics which, although constrained in their pertaining to a variedly polarized energy field, allow several modes of experience.[5] Of course, this does not amount to saying that only at a dematerialized stage of design it is possible to detect potentialities of sense to be actualized as experience, but rather that said current stage of design is the result of a process which is also historical,

---

5   For an in-depth examination of the difference between matter and material, also in connection with the creative process see Matteucci (2018: 10-2). Interestingly, in these pages he provides a particular understanding of the relationship between content and form in Adorno. He conceives of this relationship in terms of a relationship between *Gehalt* and *Gestalt* where "Ge" points to an act of "keeping parts together", and they imply

which means that in it meanings and modes from its objectual phase are sedimented with all their peculiarities.

As previously outlined, this issue can be investigated within the context of the origins of design in 1851. There, the controversial nature of design — eluding easy examination and univocal definition — finds its roots and from there develops along the whole twentieth and twenty-first century. Its development takes place between the two poles generally and canonically marked by the concepts of "function" and "form". It has however become clear that the main point is something other than this conventional couple of concepts. Their combination shows in fact that, from the start, design has had — and still has — the profiling of experiences at its core. In this regard, the current label "Experience Design" should not sound redundant, but rather as the radicalization of this distinctive feature of design in general.

This has become even clearer as, fuelled by a special development of HCI between the 1980s and the 1990s, an increasingly explicit thematization of design as design of experience has come to the fore.

It is worth remarking that the several steps accounting for the historical trajectory of design, as well as for the variable historical specification of the issue of the design of experience, are generally seen as coinciding with the main phases of aestheticization. These are the openings of Department stores and International exhibitions, broadly speaking matching the *Jugendstil* era; the progressive intertwining of technology, art, and mass consumption established in the early decades of the twentieth century; pop culture; and the virtual–digital revolution. Needless to say, Adorno has been witness to all these stages — sometimes to their later developments, sometimes to the phenomena themselves as they were happening — except the one where the digital component is significantly dominant. However, as already pointed out concerning Dewey, also Adorno could identify key aspects that were to surface in that phase already several decades before their full configuration. This cannot but confirm the great prognostic value of both philosophers' contributions.

---

totalities, rather than in terms of *Inhalt* and *Form* where, contrariwise, a distinction between elements is possible, as they are "detachable".

The digital component of design, notably in the light of what the third wave of HCI development has brought about, has given relevance to the growing attempts to conceptualize not easily quantifiable elements, by embracing a more holistic and environmental approach, as well as to the growing attempts by designers to define what experience is. And this is not an easy task.

Adorno comes here in handy, when he describes the failure and the negativity of the concept in experience. The concept becomes, within Adorno's project, a properly aesthetic concept, inasmuch as experience can be fully achieved only as highest achievement of energy, and its qualities and distinctive features do not lend themselves to be fully subsumed under, nor formatted according to, a transparent and univocal realm of knowledge. One should therefore distinguish, as already widely attempted in this essay, the thematic component and the operative, immersive component of design. What gets each time thematized by design are only some aspects of experience, since through experiential configurations design can only intensify the operative aspects that are implicitly or immanently sedimented, in force at a material level, which are in themselves unavailable to thematization and can therefore only be operatively actualized.

> The specifically artistic achievement is an overarching binding character to be ensnared not thematically or by the manipulation of effects but rather by presenting what is beyond the monad through immersion in the experiences that are fundamental to this bindingness. The result of the work is as much the trajectory it traverses to its imago as it is the imago itself as the goal; it is at once static and dynamic. (Adorno 1970: 86)

It is not a coincidence that in the third wave of research in HCI an essential shift has occurred from "pure and simple" Usability, that is, "chemically pure purposefulness", as Adorno would say, to User Experience. This transition coincides with a general tendency to overcome a minimalist approach, geared to an ideal and ideological cognitivist simplicity defining, notably, Usability, and place value instead on features that can be referred back to the realm of the aesthetic. Usability would then be the "correlate" of a "Loos-like" functionalist approach, demonizing the "ornament" regardless of the meaning it may take on in a given context. This transition, moreover, is important inasmuch as it acknowledges, first, that any approach to design which fails to take into account also more gratifying aspects, connected to some kind of pleasure, has limited efficacy, and, second, that it is possible to leverage on those aspects in order to make an experience work and fuel it and sustain it according to the immanent logic of its field. A move made by a scholar as attentive to issues such as design and sustainability as Yuriko Saito can also be recalled in this context. In Saito (2018), addressing the delicate issue of the aesthetics of sustainable consumption, she partially revises her theoretical proposal for a green aesthetics elaborated in Saito (2007). She no longer univocally focuses on specific characteristics (such as, for instance, minimalism) that a designed object should have in order to be sustainable, but emphasizes the centrality of the relationship between human beings and the material world as such.

However, the already discussed further shift from User Experience Design to Experience Design indicates that design has acknowledged a certain degree of responsibilization to the user, now perceived as an integrated vector in the experience itself, and not as the mere "target" of a designed device. To the hyper-functional experiential field of Experience Design correspond indeed users who are hyper-consumers. In the persisting of their aesthetic field, these latter find their actualization of aesthetic reflectivity, as reflectivity internal to the material itself.

A negative connotation can end up being attached to this, whenever a pre-ordering of all behaviors of the aesthetic consumer is implied. A positive connotation ensues instead when the experience with the device becomes an intensification of one's existence and reflectivity, even leading to an emancipatory outcome. This corresponds precisely to what Adorno points out in the concluding section of the essay on functionalism this chapter has started from.

As already made clear in the first chapter, from the point of view of design, all this is based on a specific assumption. The course of the previously described immersive and interactive experience hinges upon, or better, relies on an implicit competence that is given for granted. Here, in Adorno's terms, one could identify it as mimetic.

3.4. *Aesthetic Competence: from Nature to Nature. And Back*

> Every artwork is in fact an oxymoron. Its own reality is for it unreal, it is indifferent to what it essentially is, and at the same time it is its own precondition; in the context of reality it is all the more unreal and chimerical. The enemies of art have always understood this better than those of its apologists who have fruitlessly sought to deny its constitutive paradox. Aesthetics is powerless that seeks to dissolve the constitutive contradiction rather than conceiving of art by way of it. (Adorno 1970: 279)

This passage from *Aesthetic Theory* seems to frame precisely the above outlined issue concerning the constitutive, distinctive, although after all only apparent, oxymoronic nature of Experience Design. The processual perspective applied to the investigation of experience and identity has indeed yielded an idea of experience featuring the threshold where all antinomic elements are at play, and proving the untenability of a mere opposition between artificiality and naturality. To say it better, that relationship has turned out to be a rather peculiar one, as, in actual terms, as previously shown, the more Experience Design makes what is artificial ("the unreality") appear natural ("the reality"), or even, the more it is able to design happy (that is, immediate) interactions that are not simple (that is, mediated), the more it comes out as successful, hence cool.

> The reality and unreality of artworks are not layers superimposed on each other; rather, they interpenetrate everything in art to an equal degree. An artwork is real only to the extent that, as an artwork, it is unreal, self-sufficient, and differentiated from the empirical world, of which it nevertheless remains a part. (Adorno 1970: 279)

The same point is repeated in the following passage, where more can be learnt about the oscillation between individuality and society, between emergence and integration.

> But its unreality — its determination as spirit — only exists to the extent that it has become real; nothing in an artwork counts that is not there in an individuated form. In aesthetic semblance

the artwork takes up a stance toward reality, which it negates by becoming a reality sui generis. (Adorno 1970: 279)

At any rate, as it facilitates for instance our everyday life, such "mediated immediacy" is, on the one hand, gratifying and endowed of a positive connotation; on the other hand, it entails less positive aspects. It can indeed convey a true loss of experience in the richest meaning of the word, in terms of a lack of creativity, alienation — if experience is excessively delegated — and/or as form of unsustainability and hedonism — if experience structures are ab-used — turning into something that is unsustainable both for the individual and for the environment. It is clear, then, that the thematization of Experience Design implies the thematization of rather complex issues.

Here as well, one can attempt to answer some questions formulated in the first chapter by translating them into Adorno's terms. Two main questions may suffice here: when everything has been designed, and our everyday environment is saturated by pre-established experiential frameworks, what is left of the individual ability to generate new meanings, hence being creative, making a difference, and, as Adorno would put it, being increasingly qualitatively "differentiated"? How is aesthetic sustainability achievable in the relation — that is to say, both in the construction of one's identity and towards the "other" — with designed environments? In other words, how to be responsible in a way that is also gratifying?

An answer to these questions can be formulated starting from the following passage in Adorno's text: "culture is not the place for untamed nature, nor for a merciless domination over nature" (Adorno 1966: 8). Here, a clear summary is provided of the antinomic poles identified by Adorno as typical of the life context he is committed to account for. On the one hand, the indecency of the untamed abandoning of oneself to sensual immediate pleasures — which denies the essential historicity of experience; on the other hand, the total hegemony of *ratio* over the environment — mercilessness ensuing from the, at least alleged, generalization of the particularity of sensory aesthetic qualities.

This seems to recall a fictitious and equally ideological alternative that today, in the world of global design, re-emerges also with respect to the identification of an aesthetics that responsibly takes on the environmental challenge. If it is in fact true that a mere aesthetic hedonism can only be devastating in its environmental impact, it is also true that its antidote cannot be the proclamation of absolute ecological and environmental values. The intrinsic limit of the latter would be, in fact, their mortification of forms of aestheticity and gratification as such. This is clearly shown by the proposal put forward in Saito (2007) and yet partly revised, as seen above, in Saito (2018). However, Saito (2007: 88–96) maintains that such values as minimalism; durability and longevity; fittingness, appropriateness and site-specificity; valuing the contrast between past and present; perceivability of nature's function; health; caring and sensitive attitude, if stressed and employed in consumerist contexts, but also if learnt to be appreciated aesthetically as embodying environmental value, could contribute to the furtherment of a more sustainable ("greener") aesthetics.

Contra Saito, a more "anti-essentialist", fluid, so to speak, stance, which also embraces the antinomic reality of phenomena is Ossi Naukkarinen's. Although he recognizes (just like we do) the importance and relevance of the issues Saito takes up, not the least because they try to find concrete solutions to concrete problems, and that they deserve serious attention, he states that Saito's proposal may not be as effective as she hopes. Among other critical points he identifies in it, Naukkarinen maintains that some of the features Saito advocates (again, such as minimalism but also durability) in her project of a green aesthetics can be exactly measured or quantified, generalized, hence are not *specifically* aesthetic, they do not promote the particular, first-hand experience which connotes the aesthetic dimension.

> If we talk about *aesthetic evaluation* we have quite another type of issue at hand. It is not self-evident at all that *any* aesthetic feature can be expressed, embodied, or revealed in a simple and indisputable manner and we cannot be sure to whom it may be, say, attractive if it is perceived. (Naukkarinen 2011: 107)

In Adorno such aesthetic features are also those rejected by Loos in his project of ideological functionalization of reality. Loos namely represses the ornament based on its connection to the erotic, and in so doing equally represses any *élan*, any striving towards alterity. As a result, though, also one of the fundamental hinges of the aesthetic and art — one of the pillars of Adorno's theory on aesthetic and artistic experience — is repressed, that is to say, mimesis.

> His hatred of ornament could not be understood if he did not feel in it [*scil.*: in the ornament] the mimetic impulse, which runs contrary to rational objectification (Adorno 1966: 8)

In the essay on functionalism, the mimetic component of experience is brought into play in particular by means of the notion of *Zweckform*, purposeful form:

> purposeful forms are the language of their own purposes. By means of the mimetic impulse, the living being equates himself with objects in his surroundings. This occurs long before artists initiate conscious imitation. What begins as symbol becomes ornament, and finally appears superfluous; it had its origins, nevertheless, in natural shapes, to which men adapted themselves through their artifacts. The inner image which is expressed in that impulse was once something external, something coercively objective. (Adorno 1966: 9)

Thanks to the mimetic impulse, here acting in the functional form, as expressive and aesthetic incorporation of nature, a way out is possible, according to Adorno, both from the "untamed nature" — mediated namely through form, which is artificial — and from the "merciless domination" of nature — from which one escapes and from which nature escapes as soon as a process of incorporation and absorption becomes what fuels its inherent dynamics, hence the actualization of its sense potential. In this regard, it might be suggested that the purposeful forms, that is, the objects of use as such, are, according to Adorno, a form of adaptation, not only because they are mimesis of the natural forms they serve to incorporate, but also because they are the non-natural that notwithstanding allows the living to interact with, hence experience nature. Or better, to be nature. And whether subjectual polarization or objectual polarization, nature is always, according to Adorno, a matter of mediation.

Still, aesthetic mimesis of functionality cannot be revoked through recourse to the subjectively unmediated: This would only mask how much the individual and his psychology have become ideological with regard to the supremacy of social objectivity, a supremacy of which *Sachlichkeit* is correctly conscious. (Adorno 1970: 61)

At any rate, going back to the above mentioned passage on the purposeful forms, one can retrieve a particularly useful element. Its concluding words suggest indeed a possible direction to be applied to the previously formulated thorny questions. Adorno says: "ornament, indeed artistic form in general, cannot be invented" (Adorno 1966: 9).[6] This statement concerns both the type of possible creativity in the described life context and how to try and become aesthetically competent in it. Once more, strong affinities emerge with Dewey's position.

Among the several poles of tension mentioned by Adorno in his essay, one should also refer here to two historical instances: the "handicraft" [*Handwerk*] understood as something that has undergone a barbaric denaturalization via specialization and has thereby become the unreflected generalization of the particular — Loos' orthodox functionalism; and the "imagination" [*Phantasie*]. Whenever understood as mere external corrective to the specializing drift of handicraft, imagination turns into a pure idiosyncratic "fantasy", a subjective digression, with no regard for the historicity of the materials with which it interacts, and therefore not expressing nor incorporating their instances — mere ornamentalism. The type of imagination described by Adorno has instead a clear meaning. While taking up Benjamin's account (1928: 75), he defines it as the "ability to interpolate in the minutest detail" (Adorno 1966: 12), a micrological exercise.[7]

Psychological triviality [says that] imagination [is] nothing but the image of something not yet present [but actually it] is not pleasure in free invention, in creation *ex nihilo*. There is no such thing in

6   Here we find again the already mentioned impossibility to reduce invention and innovation in design.

7   This same idea could be compared to the terms in which Maskit (2011) has described an "Aesthetics of Elsewhere" and Naukkarinen (2011) an "Aesthetic Footprint". They both imply the ability to orient present

any art, even in autonomous art, the realm to which Loos restricted imagination. [...] Clearly there exists, perhaps in the materials and forms which the artist acquires and develops something more than material and forms. Imagination means to innervate this something [more]. (Adorno 1966: 12)

This creativity is tied to the already existing and sustainable, as it is attentive to the instances expressed by the context taken into account, and, while expressing them, it also incorporates them. This is, once more, not a Promethean creativity. This is enabled by an empowering competence, that is, the ability to bring forth something that cannot be reduced not even to materials and forms, but that qualifies as a "something more" which is sense connection, sense mode and sense configuration. In other words, it is the ability to create sense connections, "as little as they still make sense",[8] between poles with different but equally in force instances.

The great utopian project of the aesthetic advocated by Adorno seems then to emerge, surprisingly, and yet clearly dialectically, precisely in those forms of aestheticity that are most compromised (such as fashion, and, in this case, the design of experience), inasmuch as the radical dwelling in, or inhabiting, the material makes the possibility stand out. Whenever simply announced and opposed to reality, the escaping route is sterile and easily prone to marketing. As soon as two poles are considerably detached and sclerotized, they turn into an object, a commodity that can be sold (just like Dewey's "bare geometric figure"). More much fruitful is to look for that tiny grain eluding the mechanism and stalling it. And this is so in the most important respect.

The comparison between fine — autonomous — arts and applied — heteronomous — arts shows then how, at variance with the belief that art must be function-less, precisely because it actually

---

(aesthetic) action by taking into account how this action may have an impact on the aesthetics of another place at any given time. These notions are clearly in dialogue with ecological and environmental takes on aesthetics. A further ethically oriented understanding of "imagination" in a Deweyan key is Fesmire (2003).

8   Please note that this passage: "So wenig sie noch sinnhaft sind" has been translated as "perhaps imperceptible" in the English version.

has a function, which is that of finding self-realization, it is able to unhinge the mechanism. It is therefore not non-design to be important, but rather hyper-design, as the enhancing of an intra-experiential, monadic function, in the particular sense described by Adorno. So, a sudden glow reveals the persistent underlying presence of the mimetic — which underpins also Adorno's always rigorously dialectical theory of aura. What emerges is repressed spontaneity, which therefore must also be relying on the mimetic. At least in the form of potential, it emerges in the minuscule surviving margins, in the "minutest detail", which is namely that "something more" to be innervated, as Adorno suggests, "with imagination".

In its utmost effort as design of experience, design discovers that the positive outcome of the whole enterprise lies in the hands of the users. In this sense, unlike what it seemed at first, rather than overriding their aesthetic competence, it emphasizes it. In this effort of "ultimate" design, its implicit core, that is the mimetic attitude of the aesthetic, its style, is revealed. This could be read as a new release of the natural, resulting from its sudden irruption within the artificial, as the glow of a primordial mimetic attitude. All this, clearly, provided design does not saturate every experiential space by mechanically pre-establishing each and every one of its modules. This would however qualify as designed experience more than as experience design, turning the aesthetic potential nested at its core into total alienation — as the pure market logic currently in force seems to wish, despite making experience of its intrinsic contradiction by generating simultaneously the key to its potential radical disassembling.

Within Experience Design, construction is never enough, because something irreducible is there that is not construction, in other words, the mimetic attitude as competence for the absorption of and the interaction with the environment. This latter is a relation of material embodiment, not of transcendence, inasmuch as it coincides with engendering and configuring something by expressing its immanent function. As it is based on the aesthetic competence of living organisms understood as mimetic competence in relation to their environment, this relation qualifies also as sustainable.

Precisely when it seems that everything has turned into artifice, the firework of nature appears. Everything is indeed based on a connection of global interaction, a field connection, which qualifies as mimetic naturality. Here the dialectical process is fully achieved. This is the dialectics of construction, that is to say, the dialectics of functionalism. From nature to nature. And back.

CONCLUSION
STYLE OF THE IMPLICIT

The questions that have oriented the course of this essay have searched for answers in two apparently irreconcilable perspectives such as those of John Dewey and Theodor W. Adorno. A supposedly complete irreconcilability of these two perspectives seems to have been largely proved wrong. Several commonalities between Dewey and Adorno have been identified in the analysis of some of their works dedicated to the treatment of the aesthetic and aesthetics according to the relationship between form and function. Each of these philosophers evidently has a particular and chosen "prop" for unhinging ideal or non-historical, dichotomous or dualistic, ideological or orthodox conceptions of the relationship between form and function. In Dewey's case, the emphasis is in particular on a form that has to do with operativity, with the functionality of experience. In Adorno's case the emphasis is on a function that emerges as a form of experience. However, each preference, so to speak, does not contradict Dewey's and Adorno's aim of constantly bringing to the fore the continuity that runs between form and function. Both texts are examples of an anti-dualist philosophical attitude able to "keep things together" especially when they are intrinsically antinomic. An ability, the latter, that today more than ever seems to be required by the particular historical context in which we are situated, and which has in Experience Design an excellent exemplary incarnation.

Should we want to summarize under a label, perhaps even a little evocative one, the core of this commonality, one could speak of a "Style of the Implicit". One could speak of the latter in terms of something that emerges even when everything seems to be rigidly quantified, pre-packaged and pre-constituted. It is a pervasively operative substratum of qualitative irreducibility that emerges and proves capable of escaping any domestication. At the same time, though, it does not evade the direct involvement with current reality, and therefore it does not ideologically reject it, however designed it may be. It is a style that implies the ability to manage reality in the best possible way for how it offers itself. With all its facilitations and all its constraints. With all its contradictions. In Dewey it is specified as a style of perception: it is the repleteness of sense expressed by a situation and which is grasped, absorbed and re-issued into the world; in Adorno it is specified as a style of the mimetic attitude: it is the repressed element of spontaneity, of the natural that manifests itself.

A style is personal: it distinguishes, and at the same time it is general, it brings together; a style concerns the emotional dimension, insofar as it corresponds to a perception of the self with respect to the object, event or situation in which it operates and interacts; a style is a "stance" of some kind towards what we experience, it is a particular form of judgment that is expressed not necessarily at a propositional level, but often coincides with behaviors, choices and ways of life; a style has a dynamic regulativity: we acquire it by being immersed in the environments we grow in and in the course of our lives, and hence it is processual, it can be learned, it is oriented by our expectations, and yet, in this sense, it is also bound to use and context. Thus, the peculiarity of this normativity is that it is a dynamic one, it works well even in the absence of "instruction manuals" or "guides" that explicitly explain how it should be carried out. It is a style of the implicit understood as a style of what is potential and unexpressed, even repressed. It is a style of the implicit understood as a style of what is unquestioned, taken for granted, of the material reality with which we relate. In the interaction between organism and environment it is the style of implicitly, operatively active vectors that mutually makes the style of implicitly, operatively active vectors more perspicuous, more conspicuous. It has to do with that perception–expression nexus dear to Dewey, and to that movement "from nature to nature, and back" we glimpsed in Adorno. It has to do with that complex field of Experience Design where producers, users and environments are together. Then, if it is true that the "anti-essentialist" markers of the aesthetic mentioned at the beginning of this essay — and just recalled in order to describe the characters of a style — are indicators of a qualitatively dense situation just like a situation in which the aesthetic is involved can be, this style could be defined as a style of the aesthetic.

In this framework, Experience Design considered in the terms we proposed, i.e. as a design that is not "prescriptive", or at least not perceived as such, but "inviting", has proved to be an important element of exemplification of this "mutual stylistic nexus". In making available thematized and intensified functions in yet pre-determined forms, however, it has recognized a fundamental role for the aesthetic user. It has recognized her/his role as a competent individual who is necessary for the success of the experiential field meant as an experiential field that can become one's own, identitary but shared, inhabitable and irreducibly human. An experiential field in which one could keep things together, nicely.

BIBLIOGRAPHY

For all the works quoted in the essay the indication of the year of the original edition (located in the bibliography immediately after the author's name) has been kept, while for the page number (when needed) we referred readers to the edition or translation actually used and properly referenced in the bibliography after the publisher's name.

Adler, Hans (ed.). 2002. *Aesthetics and Aisthesis: New Perspectives and (Re)Descoveries* (Oxford: Peter Lang)

Adorno, Theodor W. (1966) 'Functionalism Today', in *Rethinking Architecture: A Reader in Cultural Theory*, ed. by Neil Leach (London-New York: Routledge, 1997), pp. 5–18

——(1970) *Aesthetic Theory* (London-Boston: Routledge and Kegan Paul, 1984)

——1977. 'Ohne Leitbild. Anstelle einer Vorrede', in *Gesammelte Schriften*, vol. 10/1 (Frankfurt a. M.: Suhrkamp), pp. 291–301

Agamben, Giorgio. 2006. *Che cos'è un dispositivo?* (Roma: Nottetempo)

Alexander, Thomas. 1987. *John Dewey's Theory of Art, Experience and Nature: The Horizons of Feeling* (Albany, NY: SUNY Press)

Auerbach, Jeffrey A., and Peter H. Hoffenberg (eds.). 2016. *Britain, the Empire, and the World at the Great Exhibition of 1851* (London-New York: Routledge)

Barnard, Malcolm. 1996. *Fashion as Communication* (London: Routledge)

Basalla, George (ed.). 1988. *The evolution of technology* (Cambridge: Cambridge University Press)

Benjamin, Andrew. 2000. *Allowing Function Complexity. Notes on Adorno's 'Functionalism Today'*, AA Files, 41: 40–5

Benjamin, Walter (1928) *One-Way Street* (London: NLB, 1975)

——(1938) 'On Some Motifs on Baudelaire', in *The Writer of Modern Life. Essays on Charles Baudelaire*, ed. by Michael W. Jennings (Cambridge, MA-London: The Belknap Press of Harvard University Press, 2006), pp. 171–210

Benz, Peter (ed.). 2015. *Experience Design: Concepts and Case Studies* (London-New York: Bloomsbury)

Betts, Paul. 2007. *The Authority of Everyday Things. A Cultural History of West German Industrial Design* (Oakland: University of California Press)

Bhatt, Ritu (ed.). 2013. *Rethinking Aesthetics: The Role of Body in Design* (London-New York: Routledge)

Blythe, Mark et al. 2009. 'Now With Added Experience?', *New Rev Hypermedia Multimed*, 15/2: 119–28

Bødker, Susanne. 2006. 'When Second Wave HCI Meets Third Wave Challenges', *Proceedings of the 4th Nordic Conference on Human-Computer Interaction: Changing Roles* (New York: ACM Press), pp. 1–8

Böhme, Gernot. 2001. *Aisthetik. Vorlesungen über Ästhetik als allgemeine Wahrnehmungslehre* (München: Wilhelm Fink)

Bony, Anne. 2005. *Design: History, Main Trends, Major Figures* (Edinburgh: Chambers)

Bonzon, Roman. 2009. 'Thick Aesthetic Concepts', *The Journal of Aesthetics and Art Criticism*, 67/2: 191–9

Bosbach, Franz, and John Davis. 2012. *Die Weltausstellung Von 1851 und Ihre Folgen* (München: K. G. Saur Verlag)

Bourdieu, Pierre (1980) *Le sens pratique, The Logic of Practice* (Stanford, CA: Stanford University Press, 1990)

——(1992) *Rules of Art: Genesis and Structure of the Literary Field* (Stanford, CA: Stanford University Press, 1996)

——(1997) *Pascalian Meditations* (Stanford, CA: Stanford University Press, 2000)

Calleja, Gordon. 2001. *In-Game. From Immersion to Incorporation* (Cambridge, MA-London: The MIT Press)

Carnevali, Barbara. 2012. *Le apparenze sociali. Una filosofia del prestigio* (Bologna: Il Mulino)

Cassirer, Ernst (1923-29) *Philosophy of Symbolic Forms*, 3 vols, (New Haven: Yale University Press, 1955-1957)

——(1930) *Form and Technology*, in *The Warburg Years (1919–1933): Essays on Language, Art, Myth, and Technology*, ed. by Steve G. Lofts, and Antonio Calcagno (New Haven-London: Yale University Press, 2013), pp. 272–316

———(1931) *Mythic, Aesthetic, and Theoretical Space*, in *The Warburg Years (1919–1933): Essays on Language, Art, Myth, and Technology*, ed. by Steve G. Lofts, and Antonio Calcagno (New Haven-London: Yale University Press, 2013), pp. 317–33

———(1932) *Language and the Construction of the World of Objects*, in *The Warburg Years (1919–1933): Essays on Language, Art, Myth, and Technology*, ed. by Steve G. Lofts, and Antonio Calcagno (New Haven-London: Yale University Press, 2013), pp. 334–62

Chiodo, Simona. 2020. 'Prometheus and the Evolution of the Relationship Between Humans and Technology', *Studi di Estetica*, 16/1: 209–28

Colomina, Beatriz, and Mark Wigley. 2017. *Are We Human? Notes on an Archaeology of Design* (Baden: Lars Müller Publishers)

Cova, Bernard, and Christian Svanfeldt. 1993. 'Societal Innovations and the Postmodern Aestheticization of Everyday Life', *International Journal of Research in Marketing*, 10/3: 297–310

Csikszentmihalyi, Mihaly. 1990, *Flow: The Psychology of Optimal Experience* (New York: Harper and Row)

———1996. *Creativity: Flow and the Psychology of Discovery and Invention* (New York: Harper Perennial)

———1998. *Finding Flow: The Psychology of Engagement with Everyday Life* (New York: Basic Books, New York)

De Fusco, Renato. 2012. *Filosofia del design* (Torino: Einaudi)

Deleuze, Gilles. 1989. 'Qu'est-ce qu'un dispositif?', in *Michel Foucault philosophe. Rencontre internationale. Paris*, 9-11 janvier 1988 (Paris: Seuil), pp. 185–95

Desideri, Fabrizio, and Giovanni Matteucci. 2009. 'Introduzione a Th. W. Adorno', in Theodor W. Adorno, *Teoria estetica* (Torino: Einaudi), pp. ix–xxxiv

Dewey, John (1916) *Democracy and Education*, in *The Middle Works*, vol. 9, ed. by Jo Ann Boydston, and Larry A. Hickman (Carbondale: Southern Illinois University Press, 1980 — Charlottesville, VA: InteLex Corporation, 2003)

———(1934) *Art as Experience*, in *The Later Works*, 1925-1953, vol. 10, ed. by Jo Ann Boydston, and Larry A. Hickman (Carbondale: Southern Illinois University Press, 1987 — Charlottesville, VA: InteLex Corporation, 2003)

Di Stefano, Elisabetta. 2017. *Che cos'è l'estetica quotidiana* (Roma: Carocci)

Dilthey, Wilhelm (1906), *Poetry and Experience*, in *Wilhelm Dilthey Selected Works vol. V*, ed. by Frithjof Rodi, and Rudolf A. Makkreel (Princeton, NJ: Princeton University Press, 1985)

Dilworth, John. 2001. 'Artworks versus Designs', *British Journal of Aesthetics*, 41/4: 162–77

Dissanayake, Ellen. 2003. 'The Core of Art: Making Special', *J Can Assoc Curric Stud*, 12: 13–38

Dorst, Kees. 2006. 'Design Problems and Design Paradoxes', *Design issues*, 22/3: 4–17

Dowling, Christopher. 2010. 'The Aesthetics of Daily Life', *British Journal of Aesthetics*, 50/3: 225–42.

Dunne, Anthony. 2005. *Hertzian Tales: Electronic Products, Aesthetic Experience and Critical Design* (Cambridge, MA: The MIT Press)

Dunne, Anthony, and Fiona Raby. 2013. *Speculative Everything: Design, Fiction, and Social* Dreaming, Cambridge, MA: The MIT Press)

Edwards, Tim. 2011. *Fashion in Focus* (London-New York Routledge)

Fallan, Kjetil. 2010. *Design History. Understanding Theory and Method* (Oxford-New York: Berg)

Featherstone, Mike (1991) *Consumer Culture and Postmodernism* (London: SAGE, 2007)

Feige, Daniel Martin. 2018. *Design. Eine philosophische Analyse* (Berlin: Suhrkamp)

Fellmann, Ferdinand. 1983. *Gelebte Philosophie in Dewutschland. Denkformen der Lebenswelt-phänomenologie und der kritische Theorie* (Alber: Freiburg)

Fesmire, Steven. 2003. *John Dewey and Moral Imagination. Pragmatism in Ethics* (Bloomington, IN: Indiana University Press)

Finkelstein, Joanne. 1991. *The Fashioned Self* (London: Polity)

Fischer-Lichte, Erika. 2008. *The Transformative Power of Performance: a New Aesthetics* (London-New York: Routledge)

Flusser, Vilém (1993) *The Shape of Things. A Philosophy of Design* (London: Reaktion Books, 1999)

Folkmann, Mads Nygaard. 2013. *The Aesthetics of Imagination in Design* (Cambridge, MA: The MIT Press)

Forlizzi, Jodi. 2010, 'All Look Same?: A Comparison of Experience Design and Service Design', *Interactions*, 17/5: 60–2

Formis, Barbara. 2010. *Esthétique de la vie ordinaire* (Paris: PUF)

Forsey, Jane. 2013. *The Aesthetics of Design* (Oxford-New York: Oxford University Press)

——2014. 'The Promise, the Challenge, of Everyday Aesthetics', *Aisthesis. Pratiche, Linguaggi e Saperi dell'Estetico*, 7/1: 5–21

——2015. 'Form and Function: The Dependent Beauty of Design', *Proceedings of the European Society for Aesthetics*, vol. 7, pp. 210–20

Foster, Hal. 2002. *Design & Crime* (New York: Verso Books)

Foucault, Michel (1975) *Discipline and Punish: The Birth of the Prison* (New York: Random House, 1977)

Francalanci, Ernesto L. 2006. *Estetica degli oggetti* (Bologna: Il Mulino)

Gadamer, Hans-Georg (1960) *Truth and Method* (London: Sheed and Ward, 1989)

Goodman, Nelson. 1978. *Ways of Worldmaking* (Indianapolis: Hackett Publishing)

Greenhalgh, Paul. 1988. *Ephemeral Vistas: The "Expositions Universelles," Great Exhibitions and World's Fairs, 1851–1939,* (Manchester: Manchester University Press; distributed by St. Martin's Press, New York)

Griffero, Tonino. 2007. 'Teorie del Design', in *Dizionario di estetica,* ed. by Gianni Carchia, and Paolo D'Angelo (Roma-Bari: Laterza)

——2019. *Places, Affordances, Atmospheres. A Pathic Aesthetics* (London-New York: Routledge)

Grinnell, Joseph. 1914. *An Account of the Mammals and Birds of the Lower Colorado Valley* (Berkeley: University of California Publications in Zoology)

Haapala, Arto. 2005. 'On the Aesthetics of the Everyday: Familiarity, Strangeness, and the Meaning of Place', in *The Aesthetics of Everyday Life,* ed. by Andrew Light, and Jonathan Smith (New York: Columbia University Press), pp. 39–55

——2017. 'The Everyday, Building, and Architecture: Reflections on the Ethos and Beauty of our Built Surroundings', *Cloud-Cuckoo-Land: International Journal of Architectural Theory,* 22/36: 171–82

Hamilton, Andy. 2011. 'The Aesthetics of Design', in *Fashion — Philosophy for Everyone: Thinking with Style,* ed. by Jessica Wolfendale, and Jeannette Kennett (Malden-Oxford: Wiley-Blackwell), pp. 51–69

Hamilton, Richard (1960) 'Art and Design (Popular Culture and Personal Responsibility)', in *Collected Words* (London: Thames and Hudson, 1982), pp. 151–6

Hassenzahl, Marc. 2008. 'Aesthetics in Interactive Products: Correlates and Consequences of Beauty', in *Product Experience,* ed. by Hendrik N. J. Schifferstein, and Paul Hekkert (San Diego, CA: Elsevier), pp. 287–302

——2010. *Experience Design: Technology for All the Right Reasons* (San Rafael: Morgan & Claypool Publishers)

——2003. 'The Thing and I: Understanding the Relationship Between User and Product', in *Funology: from Usability to*

Enjoyment, ed. by Mark Blythe, and Andrew F. Monk (Dordrecht: Kluwer), pp. 31–42

Hassenzahl, Marc, and Noam Tractinsky. 2006. 'User Experience — a Research Agenda' [Editorial], *Behavior & Information Technology*, 25: 91–7

Heidegger, Martin (1935-36) 'The Origin of the Artwork', in *Martin Heidegger: The Basic Writings* (New York: Harper Collins, 1993), pp. 139–212

Hickman, Larry. 2001. *Philosophical Tools for Technological Culture. Putting Pragmatism to Work* (Bloomington: Indiana University Press)

Hirdina, Heinz. 2001. 'Design', in *Ästhetische Grundbegriffe: historisches Wörterbuch in sieben Bänden*, vol. 2, ed. by Karlheinz Barck et al. (Stuttgart-Weimar: J.B. Metzler Verlag), pp. 41–63

Hobhouse, Hermione. 2002. *The Crystal Palace and the Great Exhibition. Art, Science and Productive Industry: A History of the Royal Commission for the Exhibition of 1851* (London: Bloomsbury)

Hornbæk, Kasper, Aske Mottelson, Jarrod Knibbe, and Daniel Vogel. 2019. "What Do We Mean by 'Interaction'? An Analysis of 35 Year of CHI", in *ACM Transactions on Computer-Human Interaction*, 26/4: 1–30

Hutchison, G. Evelyn. 1957. 'Concluding Remarks', in *Special Issue, Population Studies: Animal Ecology and Demography. Cold Spring Harbor Symposia on Quantitative Biology*, 22: 415–27

Iannilli, Gioia Laura. 2014. 'Interfacing Everydayness. From Distance to Use, Through the Cartographic Paradigm', *Aisthesis. Pratiche, Linguaggi e Saperi dell'Estetico*, 7/1: 63–72

——2019a. *L'estetico e il quotidiano. Design, Everyday Aesthetics, Esperienza* (Milano-Udine: Mimesis)

——2019b. 'Towards a Reconception of the Polarity Between Aesthetics and Economics. Introductory Remarks', *Studi di Estetica*, 15/3: 1–19

Iannilli, Gioia Laura, and Stefano Marino (eds.). 2020. "Proceedings of the Conference 'Be Cool! Aesthetic Imperatives and Social Practices'", *ZoneModa Journal Special Issue*, 10/1

Ihde, Don. 2010. *Heidegger's Technologies: Postphenomenological Perspectives* (New York: Fordham University Press)

Irvin, Sherri. 2009. 'Aesthetics of Everyday Life', in *Blackwell Companions to Philosophy. A Companion to Aesthetics*, ed. by Steven Davies, et al. (Malden-Oxford: Wiley-Blackwell), pp. 136–9

Johnson, Robert Vincent. 1969. *Aestheticism* (London: Methuen)

Johnson, Mark. 2018. *The Aesthetics of Meaning and Thought. The Bodily Roots of Philosophy, Science, Morality, and Art* (Chicago-London, University of Chicago Press)

Johnson, Roswell H. 1910. *Determinate Evolution in the Color-Pattern of the Lady-Beetles* (Washington D.C.: Carnegie Institution of Washington)

Jordan, Patrick W. 1998. *An Introduction to Usability* (Boca Raton, FL: CRC Press)

Katz, Barry. 2019. "Functionalism Yesterday, Functionalism Today, Functionalism Tomorrow: Thoughts Inspired by Adorno's Address to the Deutscher Werkbund, 'Funktionalismus Heute', Delivered in Berlin on October, 3, 1965", in *Reading Adorno. The Endless Road*, ed. by Amirhosein Khandizaji (Palgrave Macmillan: London), pp. 233–45

Kendal, Jeremy, Jamshid J. Tehrani, and John Odling-Smee. 2011. 'Human Niche Construction in Interdisciplinary Focus', in *Philosophical Transactions of the Royal Society*, 366: 785–92

Kuutti, Kari. 2001. 'Hunting For the Lost User: From Sources of Errors to Active Actors — and Beyond', *Paper Presented at the Cultural Usability Seminar, Media Lab, University of Art and Design, Helsinki, April 4, 2001*

Kyndrup, Morten. 2008. "Aesthetics and Border lines. 'Design' as a Liminal Case", *The Nordic Journal of Aesthetics*, 35: 24–31

Leddy, Thomas. 1995. "Everyday Surface Aesthetic Qualities: 'Neat', 'Messy', 'Clean', 'Dirty'", *The Journal of Aesthetics and Art Criticism*, 53/3: 259–68

——2012. *The Extraordinary in the Ordinary: The Aesthetics of Everyday Life* (Peterborough: Broadview Press)

——2018. 'Saito and Thick vs. Thin Appreciation', http://aestheticstoday.blogspot.com/2018/05/saito-and-thick-vs-thin-appreciation.html

Lees-Maffei, Grace. 2014. 'Design: History and Theory', in *Encyclopedia of Aesthetics*, ed. by Mike Kelly (Oxford-New York: Oxford University Press), pp. 350–4

Lehtinen, Sanna. 2013. 'Personal Space and the Everyday Aesthetic Experience — Chasing after Boundaries and Definitions', *Paper presented at the 19th International Congress of Aesthetics — Aesthetics in Action, Krakow, Poland, July 21-27, 2013*

Light, Andrew, and Jonathan Smith (eds.). 2005. *The Aesthetics of Everyday Life* (New York: Columbia University Press)

Lipovetsky, Gilles. 2006. *Le bonheur paradoxal. Essay sur la société d'hyperconsommation* (Paris: Gallimard)

Lipovetsky, Gilles, and Jean Serroy. 2013. *L'esthétisation du monde: vivre à l'âge du capitalisme artiste* (Paris: Gallimard)

Livingston, Paisley. 2012. 'New Directions in Aesthetics', in *The Continuum Companion to Aesthetics* ed. by Anna Christina Ribeiro (London-New York: Continuum), pp. 255–67

Long, Christopher. 1997. 'Ornament, Crime, Myth, and Meaning', *Architecture: Material and Imagined. Proceedings of the 85th ACSA Conference* (Washington DC: ACSA Press), pp. 440–5

Loos, Adolf (1908) 'Ornament and Crime', in *Programs and Manifestos on 20th-Century Architecture*, ed. by Ulrich Conrad (Cambridge, MA: The MIT Press, 1970), pp. 19–24

Lurie, Alison. 1981. *The Language of Clothes* (London: Heinemann)

MacBride, Fraser, and John Haldane (eds.). 2018. 'The Aesthetics of Everyday Life', *The Monist*, 101/1

Malafouris, Lambros. 2013. *How Things Shape the Mind. A Theory of Material Engagement* (Cambridge, MA-London: The MIT Press)

Maldonado, Tomás, and Gui Bonsiepe. 1964. 'Wissenschaft und Gestaltung', in *Ulm*, 10–11

Mandoki, Katia. 2007. *Everyday Aesthetics: Prosaics, the Play of Culture, and Social Identities*, (Aldershot: Ashgate)

Manovich, Lev. 2019. *AI Aesthetics* (Moskow: Strelka Press)

Marfia, Gustavo, and Giovanni Matteucci. 2018. 'Some Remarks on Aesthetics and Computer Science', *Studi di Estetica*, 12/3: 1–30

Margolin, Victor. 1997. 'Getting to Know the User', *Design Studies*, 18/3: 227–36

——2014. *World History of Design*, vol. I (London: Bloomsbury)

Marolda, Paolo. 1994. *Linguaggio ed estetica in Dewey. Le condizioni non logiche dell'esperienza* (Arezzo: Edizioni M.E.M)

Maskit, Jonathan. 2011. 'The Aesthetics of Elsewhere: An Environmentalist Everyday Aesthetics', *Aesthetic Pathways*, 1/2: 92–107

Matté Ganet, Leslie. 2017. 'Experience Design: Explanation and Best Practices', in *Designing Interactive Hypermedia Systems*, ed. by Everardo Reyes-Garcia, and Nasreddine Bouhaï (London, Hoboken: ISTE, John Wiley & Sons), pp. 97–129

Matteucci, Giovanni. 2015. *Il sensibile rimosso. Itinerari di estetica sulla scena americana* (Milano-Udine: Mimesis)

——2016. 'The Aesthetic as a Matter of Practices: Form of Life in Everydayness and Art', *Comprendre*, 18/2: 9–28

——2017. 'Everyday Aesthetics and Aestheticization: Reflectivity in Perception', *Studi di Estetica*, 7/3: 207–27

──2018. *Il jazz in Adorno: variazioni in serie*, in Theodor W. Adorno, *Variazioni sul Jazz*, (Milano-Udine: Mimesis), pp. 2–22

──2019. *Estetica e natura umana. La mente estesa tra percezione, emozione ed espressione* (Roma: Carocci)

──2020, 'How Many Experiences for an Extended Mind? — Book Forum On Mark Johnson's *The Aesthetics of Meaning and Thought*', *Studi di Estetica*, 16/1: 312–8

McCarthy, John, and Peter Wright. 2004. *Technology as experience* (Cambridge, MA-London: The MIT Press)

Mecacci, Andrea. 2012. *Estetica e design* (Bologna: Il Mulino)

──2017. *Dopo Warhol. Il pop, il postmoderno, l'estetica diffusa* (Roma: Donzelli Editore)

Melchionne, Kevin. 2014. 'The Point of Everyday Aesthetics', *Contemporary Aesthetics*, 11, https://contempaesthetics.org/newvolume/pages/article.php?articleID=700&searchstr=melchionne

──2017. 'Aesthetic Choice', *British Journal of Aesthetics*, 57/3: 283–98

Menary, Richard. 2014. 'The Aesthetic Niche', *British Journal of Aesthetics*, 54/4: 471-5

Michaud, Yves. 2003. *L'art à l'etat gazeux* (Paris: Éditions Stock)

──2013. 'Design d'objet et design d'experiénce: actualité du concept de design au delà du visible', *Figures de l'art*, ed. by Bernard Lafargue, and Stéphanie Cardoso, 25: 399–409

Midal, Alexandra. 2020. *Design by Accident. For a New History of Design* (Berlin: Sternberg Press)

Mitcham, Carl. 2001. 'Dasein versus Design: The Problematics of Turning Making into Thinking', *International Journal of Technology and Design Education*, 11/1: 27–36

Morozov, Evgeny. 2013. *To Save Everything Click Here. Technology, Solutionism, and the Urge to Fix Problems that Do Not Exist* (London: Penguin)

Muccioli, Cristina. 2011. *Estetica della vita quotidiana: il ricciolo di burro e altri 18 capolavori* (Milano: Abeditore)

Nanay, Bence. 2016. *Aesthetics as a Philosophy of Perception* (Oxford-London: Oxford University Press)

Naukkarinen, Ossi. 1998. *The Aesthetics of Unavoidable. Aesthetic Variation in Human Appearance* (Lahti: International Institute of Applied Aesthetics)

──2011. 'Aesthetic Footprint', *Aesthetic Pathways*, 2/1: 98–111

──2012. 'Variations in Artification', *Contemporary Aesthetics*, 4, http://www.contempaesthetics.org/newvolume/pages/article.php?articleID=635

———2013. "What is 'Everyday' in Everyday Aesthetics", *Contemporary Aesthetics*, 11, http://www.contempaesthetics.org/newvolume/pages/article.php?articleID=675

———2017. 'Everyday Aesthetics and Everyday Behavior', *Contemporary Aesthetics*, 15, https://contempaesthetics.org/newvolume/pages/article.php?articleID=802

———2019. 'Feeling (with) machines', in *Paths From the Philosophy of Art to Everyday Aesthetics*, ed. by Oiva Kuisma, Sanna Lehtinen, and Harri Mäcklin (Helsinki: University of Helsinki), pp. 180–200

———2020. *Aesthetics as Space* (Espoo: Aalto Art Books)

Naukkarinen, Ossi, and Johanna Bragge. 2016. 'Aesthetics in the Age of Digital Humanities', *Journal of Aesthetics and Culture*, 8: 1–18

Naukkarinen, Ossi, and Raine Vasquez. 2017. 'Creating and Experiencing the Everyday Through Daily Life', in *Experiencing the Everyday*, ed. by Carsten Friberg, and Raine Vasquez (Copenhagen: NSU Press), pp. 166–89

Naukkarinen, Ossi, and Darius Pacauskas. 2018. 'Aesthetics in Digital Worlds', *Contemporary Aesthetics*, 16, https://contempaesthetics.org/newvolume/pages/article.php?articleID=837

Newbery, Patrick, and Kevin Farnham. 2013. *Experience Design: A Framework for Integrating Brand, Experience and Value* (Hoboken, NJ: John Wiley & Sons)

Nida-Rümelin, Julian, and Jacob Steinbrenner. 2010. Ästhetische *Werte und Design* (München: Hatje Kantz)

Nielsen, Henrik Kaare. 2005. 'Totalizing Aesthetics? Aesthetic Theory and the Aestheticization of Everyday Life', *Nordisk Estetisk Tidskrift*, 32: 60–75

Norman, Donald A. 1998. *The Design of Everyday Things* (New York: Currency Book)

Paci, Enzo. 1957. 'Orientamento estetico relazionistico', in *Dall'esistenzialismo al relazionismo* (Messina-Firenze: D'Anna), pp. 283–98

Palmer, Jerry, and Mo Dodson. 1996. *Design and Aesthetics: A Reader* (London-New York: Routledge)

———2014. 'Design: Overview', in *Encyclopedia of Aesthetics*, ed. by Michael Kelly (Oxford-London: Oxford University Press)

Pareyson, Luigi (1954) *Estetica. Teoria della formatività* (Milano: Bompiani, 1988)

Parsons, Glenn. 2016. *Philosophy of Design* (Cambridge: Polity)

Peacocke, Christopher. 1992. 'Scenarios, Concepts and Perception', in *The Content of Experience: Essays in Perception*, ed. by Tim Crane (Cambridge-New York: Cambridge University Press), pp. 105–35

Pine II, B. Joseph, and James H. Gilmore (1999) *The Experience Economy* (Boston: Harvard Business School Press, 2011)

Poldma, Tiiu. 2016. Experience Design, in *The Bloomsbury Encyclopedia of Design*, ed. by Clive Edwards (London: Bloomsbury), pp. 496–7

Portera, Mariagrazia. 2016. 'Why Do Human Perceptions of Beauty Change? The Construction of the Aesthetic Niche', in *RCC Perspectives: Transformations in Environment and Society*, 5: 41–7

Postrel, Virginia. 2003. *The Substance of Style: How the Rise of Aesthetic Value is Remaking Commerce, Culture, and Consciousness* (New York: Harper Collins)

Puolakka, Kalle. 2014. 'Dewey and Everyday Aesthetics — A New Look', *Contemporary Aesthetics*, 12, http://contempaesthetics. org/newvolume/pages/article. php?articleID=699

——2015. 'The Aesthetic Pulse of the Everyday: Defending Dewey', *Contemporary Aesthetics*, 13, 2015, https:// www.contempaesthetics.org/newvolume/pages/article. php?articleID=730.

Ratiu, Dan Eugen. 2013. 'Remapping the Realm of Aesthetics: on Recent Controversies About the Aesthetic and Aesthetic Experience in Everyday Life', *Estetika, The Central European Journal of Aesthetics*, 6/1: 3–26

——2017. 'Everyday Aesthetic Experience: Exploration by a Practical Aesthetics', in *Experiencing the Everyday*, ed. by Carsten Friberg, and Raine Vasquez (Copenhagen: NSU Press), pp. 22–52

Rawsthorn, Alice. 2018. *Design as an Attitude* (Zurich: JRP Ringier)

Reckwitz, Andreas. 2017. *The Invention of Creativity* (Polity Press: Cambridge)

Richards, Richard A. 2017. 'Engineered Niches and Naturalized Aesthetics', *The Journal of Aesthetics and Art Criticism*, 75/4: 465–77

Rittel, Horst W.J., and Melvin M. Webber. 1973. 'Dilemmas in a General Theory of Planning', *Policy Sciences*, 4/2: 155–69

Rothenberg, Julia. 2011. 'Aestheticization of Everyday Life', in *Encyclopedia of Consumer Culture*, ed. by Dale Southerton (London: SAGE), pp. 15–21

Russell, Luke. 2011. 'Tryhards, Fashion Victims and Effortless Cool', in *Fashion — Philosophy for Everyone: Thinking with Style*, ed. by Jessica Wolfendale, and Jeannette Kennett (Malden-Oxford: Wiley-Blackwell), pp. 37–49

Saito, Yuriko. 2007. *Everyday Aesthetics* (Oxford-New York: Oxford University Press)

——2015. 'Aesthetics of Everyday Life', in *Stanford Encyclopedia of Philosophy*, http://plato.stanford.edu/entries/aestheticsofeveryday/

——2018. 'Consumer Aesthetics and Environmental Ethics: Problems and Possibilities, *The Journal of Aesthetics and Art Criticism*, 76/4: 87–95

——2017. *Aesthetics of the Familiar: Everyday Life and World Making*, (Oxford-New York: Oxford University Press)

Sartwell, Crispin. 2010. 'Aesthetics of The Everyday', in *The Oxford Handbook of Aesthetics*, ed. by Jerrold Levinson, et al. (Oxford University Press, Oxford-New York), pp. 761–70

Schmitt, Bernd Herbert. 1999. *Experiential Marketing: How to Get Customers to Sense, Feel, Think, Act, Relate* (New York: Free Press)

Schulze, Gerhard. 1992. *Die Erlebnisgesellschaft: Kultursoziologie der Gegenwart* (Frankfurt am Main-New York: Campus)

Sherer, Daniel. 2014. 'Adorno's Reception of Loos: Modern Architecture, Aesthetic Theory, and the Critique of Ornament', *Potlatch*, 3: 19–31

Shook, John R. 2000. *Dewey's Empirical Theory of Knowledge and Reality* (Nashville: Vanderbilt University Press)

Simmel, Georg (1903) 'The Metropolis and Mental Life', in *The Sociology of Georg Simmel*, ed. by Kurt H. Wolff (Glencoe, IL: The Free Press, 1950), pp. 409–24

——(1908) 'The Problem of Style', *Theory, Culture, & Society* (London-Newbury Park-Delhi: SAGE, 1991), 4: 63–71

Spence, Jocelyn. 2016. *Performative Experience Design* (Berlin-Heidelberg: Springer)

Suckow, Michael. 2006. Design, in *Metzler Lexikon Ästhetik: Kunst, Medien, Design und Alltag*, ed. by Joachim Trebeß (Stuttgart-Weimar: J. B. Metzler Verlag), pp. 78–81

Thaler, Richard H., and Cass R. Sunstein. 2008. *Nudge: Improving Decisions about Health, Wealth and Happiness* (New Haven, CT: Yale University Press)

'The Great Exhibition', *The Times*, October 13, 1851

Türcke, Christoph. 2002. *Erregte Gesellschaft. Philosophie der Sensation* (München: C. H. Beck Verlag)

van Wesemael, Pieter. 2001. *Architecture of Instruction and Delight: A Socio-historical Analysis of World Exhibitions as a Didactic Phenomenon (1798-1851-1970)* (Rotterdam: 010 Publishers)

Vermaas, Peter, and Stefan Vial (eds.). 2018. *Advancements in the Philosophy of Design* (Berlin-Heidelberg: Springer Verlag)

Vitta, Maurizio. 2011. *Il progetto della bellezza. Il design fra arte e tecnica dal 1851 a oggi* (Torino: Einaudi)

——2012. *Il rifiuto degli dei. Teoria delle belle arti industriali* (Torino: Einaudi)

——2016. *Le voci delle cose* (Torino: Einaudi)

Weitz, Morris. 1956. 'The Role of Theory in Aesthetics', in *The Journal of Aesthetics and Art Criticism*, 15/1: 27–35

Welsch, Wolfgang. 1996. 'Aestheticization Processes. Phenomena, Distinctions and Prospects', in *Theory Culture Society*, 13/1, <http://www2.uni-jena.de/welsch/papers/W_Welsch_aestheticization_processes.pdf>

Wendt, Thomas. 2015. *Design for Dasein. Understanding the Design of Experiences*, Thomas Wendt

Wittgenstein, Ludwig (1953) *Philosophical Investigations* (Hoboken, NJ: Wiley-Blackwell Publishing, 2009)

Wornum, Ralph Nicholson (1851) 'The Exhibition as a Lesson in Taste', in *The Great Exhibition. Illustrated Catalogue Published in Connection with The Art Journal (facsimile)* (New York: Bounty Books — Crown Publishers, 1970), pp. i–xxii

Young, Paul. 2009. *Globalization and the Great Exhibition. The Victorian New World Order* (London: Palgrave Macmillan)

https://medium.theuxblog.com/the-5e-experience-design-model-7852324d46c

https://uxdesign.cc/experience-design-a-new-discipline-e62db76d5ed1

https://www.foolproof.co.uk/journal/experience-design-a-definition

https://www.interaction-design.org/literature/book/the-encyclopedia-of-human-computer-interaction-2nd-ed/user-experience-and-experience-design

https://www.interaction-design.org/literature/book/the-encyclopedia-of-human-computer-interaction-2nd-ed/user-experience-and-experience-design

MIMESIS GROUP
www.mimesis-group.com

MIMESIS INTERNATIONAL
www.mimesisinternational.com
info@mimesisinternational.com

MIMESIS EDIZIONI
www.mimesisedizioni.it
mimesis@mimesisedizioni.it

ÉDITIONS MIMÉSIS
www.editionsmimesis.fr
info@editionsmimesis.fr

MIMESIS COMMUNICATION
www.mim-c.net

MIMESIS EU
www.mim-eu.com

Printed by
Digital Team – Fano (PU)
June 2020